Page

Note: Sterling/ECU conversions shown in this publication are at the 30 June 1997 market rate of £1 = 1.4737 ecu.

Developments
in the
European Union

January - June 1997

Presented to Parliament by the Secretary of State
for Foreign and Commonwealth Affairs
by Command of Her Majesty
November 1997

Cm 3802

FOREWORD

Since the new Labour Government came to office, we have consistently made clear our determination to transform Britain's relations with Europe. We believe that Governments need to work together more than ever for a Europe of the people which concentrates on those issues which directly affect people's lives. The new challenges of the twenty-first century are an opportunity to shape the European Union in a way which responds to this agenda: tackling unemployment; increasing competitiveness; creating a more effective Single Market; promoting equal opportunities; fighting crime; creating a healthier environment; reforming the Common Agricultural Policy; making foreign policy coordination work better; and making a success of enlargement. All of these are themes which we expect to feature strongly during the UK's forthcoming Presidency of the European Union.

Most of the period under review in this White Paper fell under the previous Government. After our election, new Labour faced two immediate tasks: to change Britain's whole approach to Europe on the lines described above; and to adopt a more coherent and constructive policy towards the negotiations then nearing completion in the Intergovernmental Conference to revise the Treaty on European Union and the Treaty Establishing the European Community.

The Government's approach to what has since become the Treaty of Amsterdam was conditioned by the conviction that this country gets a better deal out of a constructive approach that sees the European Union as an opportunity to further the UK's interests, not as a threat to them.

The Treaty agreed by the Prime Minister and other Heads of Government at Amsterdam represents a good outcome for the UK, and an important step towards the Government's goal of a European Union that works in the interests of its citizens. All the Government's major negotiating objectives were met: in particular legal security for our frontier controls; protection of our essential interests on immigration, asylum and visa policies; a limited extension of QMV, where sensible; preservation of the veto in key areas; provision for a more effective Common Foreign and Security Policy; and a clear focus on those issues which most matter to people, such as tackling unemployment, reducing crime, promoting more openness, working for a healthier environment, combating discrimination and fighting fraud.

It is this approach - ensuring that the European Union's work reflects the concerns of the people, not the pre-occupations of the politicians - that the Government will be striving hard to take forward through the UK's Presidency in the first half of next year. If we can address the people's main worries, then we will go a long way towards modernising Europe and giving it back to the people.

Douglas Henderson

Minister of State
Foreign and Commonwealth Office

1. Summary

1.1.   The following is a summary of key developments under the Netherlands Presidency.

- **Treaty of Amsterdam.** Heads of State and Government concluded the Intergovernmental Conference (IGC) opened in 1996, and agreed a draft Treaty of Amsterdam, at the Amsterdam European Council on 16-17 June (Chapter 2).

- **Budgetary and Fraud Issues.** The Commission published its Preliminary Draft Budget for 1998 in June. In April, the Commission proposed a Preliminary Draft Supplementary and Amending Budget to the 1997 Budget mainly to budgetise the 1996 cash surplus and provide additional resources for the Commission's Consumer Policy Directorate. The Annual Report of the European Court of Auditors (ECA) on the 1995 financial year, which was published in November 1996, was discussed by ECOFIN on 17 March. In March, the then Chancellor of the Exchequer sent the Commission a response to observations made about the UK in the ECA's reports on 1995. In June, ECOFIN discussed the Eighth Annual Report from the Commission on protection of the Community's financial interests and the Fight Against Fraud. The Amsterdam European Council agreed a number of changes to the Treaty affecting financial management (Chapter 3).

- **Economic and Monetary Union.** The Amsterdam European Council agreed resolutions on the Stability and Growth Pact, Growth and Employment and the principles of a new Exchange Rate Mechanism (ERM2). The European Council endorsed the two regulations that form part of the Stability and Growth Pact for ensuring budgetary discipline in the EMU, and two regulations establishing the legal status of the euro. At Amsterdam, the European Council requested that the Council and Commission, with the co-operation of the European Monetary Institute, study effective ways of implementing the provisions of Article 109 of the Treaty and that the Council and the Commission examine and indicate how to improve the processes of economic co-ordination during stage three of EMU (Chapter 3).

- **Employment Issues.** The Amsterdam European Council agreed a new Employment Chapter for the Treaty which provides for the development of a co-ordinated strategy for employment, and that a Special European Council should be held under the Luxembourg Presidency to take forward the Amsterdam Conclusions and the Resolution agreed on Growth and Employment (Chapter 4).

- **External Relations.** The Amsterdam European Council reviewed progress on enlargement and looked forward to decisions being taken at the Luxembourg European Council on which of the candidate countries to open accession negotiations with in 1998. The EU continued negotiations with a range of third countries with a view to further liberalisation of trade. WTO negotiations on trade in telecommunications services and information technology were successfully concluded (Chapter 5).

- **Single Market.** The Action Plan for the Single Market was presented by the Commission at May's Internal Market Council and endorsed at the Amsterdam European Council. The Action Plan commits the Commission and member states to adhere to a timetable for improving the performance of the Single Market that covers the Luxembourg, UK and Austrian Presidencies (Chapter 6).

- **Agriculture and Food**. At the Agriculture Council on 17-19 March there was unanimous agreement on proposals for cattle identification and beef labelling on the basis of article 43 of the Treaty. Adoption of the cattle identification proposal will facilitate the implementation of plans to develop a fully computerised database of cattle movements in Great Britain. At the same Council the temporary rules on agrimonetary compensation were extended until January 1999. These were previously agreed at the June 1995 Agriculture Council for all member states whose agricultural conversion rates undergo appreciable revaluations, as a result of currency appreciation, before the end of April 1998. The rules protect the national currency value of the main Common Agricultural Policy (CAP) payments made direct to farmers, from the effects of revaluations within limits agreed by the Council. They also offer member states the option of compensating other income losses arising from revaluations, with up to 50 per cent reimbursement from the EU budget. In other areas, agreement was reached on agricultural support prices for 1997/98 at the Agriculture Council on 23-25 June (Chapter 7).

- **Fisheries.** On 15 April the Fisheries Council agreed the fourth Multi-Annual Guidance Programme (covering the period 1997-2001) for restructuring the fishing industry. This aims to bring fishing effort into better balance with fish stocks. During the European Council meeting in June an exchange of letters took place between the Prime Minister and the President of the Commission. This set out measures which member states may take requiring vessels bearing their flags to demonstrate that their activities contribute economic benefits for their populations dependent on fishing and related industries (Chapter 7).

- **Environment.** The Environment Council reached agreement on several important issues; including two major directives on fuel and car standards (part of the Auto-oil programme); Environmental Impact Assessment; the funding of European non-governmental organisations; the reduction in the emission of volatile organic compounds, and on the drafting, implementation and enforcement of Community environmental law. The Treaty of Amsterdam introduces a new Article requiring environmental protection to be integrated into all Community policies. The Treaty also introduces sustainable development as an objective of the Union, and extends the Codecision procedure to Article 130s(1), upon which the majority of environmental legislation is based (Chapter 8).

- **Transport.** A number of important measures were agreed, including political agreement on a regulation on new digital tachographs for commercial vehicles, and on a directive requiring ferry passenger registration. The Transport Council also agreed conclusions on Community involvement in the European Organisation for the Safety of Air Navigation (Chapter 9).

- **Energy Issues.** The Energy Council continued negotiations on a directive to liberalise the single market in gas, and adopted a Resolution on Renewable Sources of Energy. In April, the Commission produced a paper on energy policy which marked the first step towards bringing together all Community actions on energy (Chapter 10).

- **EU Funding.** New programmes were adopted covering up to 2.5 million ecu (£1.7 million) from the Structural Funds, to be made available in 1997-1999 Objective 2 areas in the UK and Gibraltar. Further progress was made in programmes to support Trans-European Networks (Chapter 11).

- **Subsidiarity and Better Regulation**. A second round of SLIM (Simpler Legislation in the Internal Market) reviews began in May and SLIM teams will provide a report on these reviews to the Internal Market Council in November. A protocol on the "Application of the Principle of Subsidiarity and Proportionality" was adopted at the IGC.

The IGC also adopted a "Declaration on the Quality of Legislation" (Chapter 12).

- **Common Foreign and Security Policy.** The CFSP agenda continued to be dominated by events in Albania, the Great Lakes Region, former Yugoslavia and the Middle East Peace Process, with the introduction of a number of new Joint Actions or Common Positions and the extension or modification of a number which had been previously agreed (Chapter 13).

- **Justice and Home Affairs.** The fight against organised crime was a major priority during the six months. The High Level Group on Organised Crime, which was set up following the Dublin European Council meeting in December 1996, drew up an Action Plan with 30 specific recommendations for carrying forward action in this field. The Action Plan was considered further by the Justice and Home Affairs Council on 28 April and approved by the Amsterdam European Council. It puts the emphasis on practical measures, including more effective implementation of existing instruments, improving co-operation with the Union's main partners, in particular the applicant countries, and balancing legislative approximation or harmonisation, where necessary, with practical co-operation between law enforcement agencies. The key role of Europol in fighting organised crime was stressed in the Action Plan. The plan also stressed the need for member states to complete ratification of the Europol Convention, so that Europol could come into operation as soon as possible. In preparation for this, two joint actions, amongst other measures, were agreed, one on how data will be stored and analysed, the other on conditions of employment for Europol staff (Chapter 14).

- **Parliamentary Scrutiny.** The House of Commons Select Committee on Procedure published a report in March on the way the House deals with European Business, and the House of Lords Select Committee on the European Communities conducted an enquiry into the scrutiny of Third Pillar documents (Chapter 15).

2.   European Councils

Noordwijk Informal European Council

2.1   On 23 May there was a special meeting of the European Council in Noordwijk to discuss progress in the Intergovernmental Conference (IGC) and prepare for its conclusion at the forthcoming European Council in Amsterdam. There were no formal Presidency conclusions, except to note that the political will existed to conclude the IGC at Amsterdam in June.

Amsterdam European Council

2.2   The European Council met in Amsterdam on 16-17 June. The main issues on the agenda were the IGC and Economic and Monetary Union (EMU). Some details on EMU and other important agenda items are given below. More detail on these and other issues discussed can be found in the relevant subject chapters in this White Paper.

2.3   Heads of State and Government successfully concluded the IGC with agreement on a draft Treaty of Amsterdam.

The Treaty of Amsterdam

The Treaty of Amsterdam amends and updates the Treaty on European Union (Maastricht), the Treaty establishing the European Community (TEC), the Treaty establishing the European Coal and Steel Community (ECSC), and the Treaty establishing the European Atomic Energy Community (EURATOM). The Treaty:

- reaffirms the importance of fundamental principles of democracy and human rights for the Union and its member states, and makes compliance with these principles an obligation for countries applying to join the Union;

- allows for sanctions to be taken against a member state which seriously and persistently breaches these fundamental principles;

- provides a legal base for Community measures to combat discrimination, subject to voting by unanimity;

- strengthens Treaty provisions on the environment, public health, and consumer policy;

- increases powers to combat fraud and waste by allowing the Council to take action by Qualified Majority Voting (QMV) to prevent and combat fraud against the

Community budget and by strengthening the powers of the Court of Auditors to investigate the use of Community funds;

- introduces a new Employment Chapter and incorporates the Social Agreement into the TEC;

- strengthens subsidiarity through a protocol enforceable in the ECJ, and provides for greater transparency in the European Union, ensuring that decision-making is more open to outside scrutiny;

- secures UK and Ireland's right to operate border controls at their frontiers;

- creates a new free movement chapter in the Community pillar, comprising asylum, immigration, and visa policy. Given their position on border controls, the UK and Ireland will not be bound by measures under this chapter, but can opt in subject to certain conditions;

- incorporates agreements reached by the 13 who are party to the Schengen agreement into the Treaties;

- makes practical improvements to the Common Foreign and Security Policy (CFSP), including a planning and analysis cell and a high representative to assist the Presidency in representation of the Union;

- introduces QMV (with a mechanism for a national veto) into CFSP for decisions implementing agreed Common Strategies;

- gives strengthened recognition to the primacy of NATO in European Defence, and includes the so-called Petersberg tasks (peace-keeping, humanitarian and crisis management) in the Treaty;

- sets out mechanisms to allow groups of member states to take forward closer co-operation amongst themselves in certain circumstances: "flexibility";

- provides for a limited further extension of QMV in the Council, and co-decision with the European Parliament;

- sets out mechanisms for future reform of the Union's institutions;

- simplifies the Treaties, bringing them up to date by the deletion of a large number of obsolete articles, and renumbers the Articles.

2.4   On EMU, the European Council agreed: a Resolution and endorsed the two Stability and Growth Pact regulations; a Resolution setting out the principles of a revamped Exchange Rate Mechanism (ERM II); regulations on the legal status of the euro; and design of euro coins. See Chapter 3. There was also agreement to hold a Special European Council on employment. See Chapter 4.

2.5   The European Council reaffirmed the importance it attaches to promoting employment. It reiterated the need for a positive and coherent approach to job creation, featuring active employment policies and the modernisation of labour markets. The European Council welcomed the interim joint report on employment prepared by ECOFIN, the Labour and Social Affairs Council and the Commission, and the progress report on the Confidence Pact on action for employment in Europe presented by the President of the Commission. More details on the new Treaty Employment Chapter agreed at the European Council can be found in Chapter 4.

2.6   The European Council also highlighted the importance of a properly functioning Single Market and welcomed the Commission's Action Plan. See Chapter 6

2.7   The European Council also invited the Commission to set up a task force to improve the quality of Community legislation and reduce the administrative burden on European business, particularly SMEs. See Chapter 12.

2.8   On Justice and Home Affairs, the European Council expressed its satisfaction with the Action Plan drawn up by the high level group on organised crime and endorsed the political guidelines submitted for its approval. The Council also stressed the key role to be played by EUROPOL in the fight against organised crime.

2.9   On the environment, the European Council reaffirmed its commitment in respect of the Earth Summit on environment and development five years ago. It also reiterated the need for a strong response to the risks of climate change.

2.10 On the external side, the European Council reviewed preparations for enlargement and considered a number of important foreign policy areas including the Middle East Peace Process, Russia and former Yugoslavia. See Chapter 5.

2.11 The European Council emphasised the importance its attaches to full respect for the rights and freedoms of the Hong Kong people and the high degree of autonomy accorded to Hong Kong under the Joint Declaration and the Basic Law of the Hong Kong Special Administrative region. See Chapter 5.

2.12 The European Council also called for renewed and sustained attention to developing responsible and coherent arms export control policy throughout the Union.

3. Economic, Budgetary and Monetary Matters

The Community Budget

3.1   The Commission published its Preliminary Draft Budget (PDB) for 1998 on 10 June. This proposes a budget of 91,307 million ecu (£61,961 million) in commitment appropriations and 84,727 million ecu (£57,496 million) in payment appropriations, respectively 3,437 million ecu (£2,332 million) and 5,854 million ecu (£3,973 million) beneath the Financial Perspective ceilings and well within the Own Resources ceiling for 1998 of 1.26 per cent of Community GNP. The PDB has been passed to the Council and European Parliament for consideration.

3.2   The Commission proposed a Preliminary Draft Supplementary and Amending Budget No 1 for 1997 on 30 April. Its main functions are to budgetise the 1996 budget underspend of 4,384 million ecu (£3,232 million[1]) and to provide additional resources for a new directorate concerning scientific opinions on health within the Commission's Directorate-General XXIV (Consumer Policy). The Council gave the Commission's proposal a first reading in June. The Draft Supplementary and Amending Budget was then passed to the European Parliament for its consideration.

3.3   On 5 May, the Commission proposal to amend the Financial Perspective to take account of the annual technical adjustment for changes to inflation and GNP growth, and conditions of implementation of the structural funds, was adopted.

Financial Management and Fraud Against Community Finances

3.4   The Annual Report of the European Court of Auditors (ECA) on the 1995 financial year, which was published in November 1996, was discussed by ECOFIN on 17 March when the Council adopted recommendations to the European Parliament on granting discharge to the Commission for execution of the 1995 Community budget. The Council recommended that discharge be granted but made a number of comments which were critical of the quality of budget execution, based on the ECA's findings. At the same time the Council adopted a statement on the ECA's annual Statement of Assurance for 1995, which was published at the same time as the Annual Report. The Statement of Assurance concerns the reliability

---

1   *Converted at the rate of £1 = £1.3564 ecu, which is the rate set for the UK's VAT and Fourth Resource contributions to the 1997 Community Budget.*

of the Community's accounts, and the legality and regularity of the underlying transactions. The Council regretted the absence, for the second year running, of a satisfactory assurance from the ECA concerning the legality and regularity of payments transactions from the Community budget; and looked forward to seeing a positive Statement of Assurance as soon as possible.

3.5   The European Parliament decided to grant the discharge to the Commission, but added its own criticisms to those made by the Council. The Commission is required to respond to the comments made by the Council and the Parliament before discharge for the 1996 budget is considered (next year).

3.6   In addition to the Annual Report of the ECA and its Statement of Assurance, the Council also considered two special reports by the ECA. One dealt with the MED programmes for co-operation with the non-EU countries of the Mediterranean region. The Council noted the suspension of the programme pending reorganisation of its management systems in response to ECA criticisms, and looked forward to a relaunch when the management reforms were complete. The other special report dealt with the EU administration in Mostar (in Bosnia-Herzegovina) where the Council noted the ECA's analysis of financial management weaknesses resulting from rapid implementation of the administration in difficult circumstances.

3.7   The ECA also published two further special reports which were too late to be considered in the discharge procedure this year - one on the Community's tourism policy and the other on the accounts of the EU Unit observing the Palestinian elections. They will be considered during the discharge procedure next year. In the first half of 1997 the ECA also published a further six special reports, which will also be considered by the Council in 1998, dealing with: the 1992 and 1993 accounts for agricultural support; humanitarian aid from 1992 to 1995; aid to central and eatern Europe; agricultural compensation in the context of German reunification; trade in cereals; and subsidies to the Ukraine.

3.8   In March, the then Chancellor of the Exchequer sent the Commission a response to observations made about the UK in the ECA's reports on 1995. There were few such observations, and only some involved criticism.

3.9   In June, ECOFIN discussed the Eighth Annual Report from the Commission on protection of the Community's financial interests and the Fight Against Fraud, dealing with 1996, together with the Commission's work programme for 1997-98 on anti-fraud measures. The statistics on fraud against the Community in 1996 showed little change from earlier years. Detected cases amounted to some 6 per cent of traditional own resources on the revenue side of the budget, and about 0.7 per cent of payments on the expenditure side of the budget. There was further evidence of the involvement of international organised crime in fraud against the Community, with 2 or 3 per cent of the cases detected accounting for over two thirds of all the money involved.

3.10   The Council endorsed the Commission's work programme, which included: establishing more central databases and co-operative task forces targeted against organised crime; improving Community legislation to minimise opportunities for fraud; and strengthening the customs transit regime (which allows for suspension of customs duties at borders for goods transiting the territory of the EU) which was heavily criticised by the European Parliament in March 1997. A Temporary Committee of Inquiry set up by the Parliament reported that the transit regime was administered with archaic inefficiency and was extremely vulnerable to abuse. The Commission has since produced an action plan for improving the system.

3.11   The Amsterdam European Council on 16-17 June agreed a number of changes to the Treaty affecting financial management, including: strengthening the role of the ECA and clarifying its rights to conduct audits; and creating for the first time a specific legal base in the Treaty for the Council to adopt anti-fraud measures. As well as agreeing to a number of proposals from the UK on audit of the Community's spending and the transparency of its financial reporting, the Summit decided to include in the Treaty the UK proposal for a legal requirement for member states to co-operate with the Commission in implementing the Community budget according to principles of 'sound financial management'.

3.12   Throughout the first half of 1997 there has been further work under Phase III of the Commission's SEM 2000 (Sound and Efficient Management) programme to improve resource management. The Group of Personal Representatives of Finance Ministers which advises the Commission produced a further six monthly report in May, which was presented to the Council by Commissioners Gradin (Financial Control) and Liikanen (Budget). In June, ECOFIN took note of the report. Amongst the priorities emphasised in the report were further work to ensure that new legislation is fraud-proofed; to improve co-ordination of financial controls, budget forecasting and evaluation of spending; and to define better the conditions for eligibility for Structural Funds spending and the treatment of spending which is found to be ineligible. A further report will be presented at the end of 1997.

Economic and Monetary Union (EMU)

3.13   The Amsterdam European Council agreed a Resolution laying down the firm commitments of the member states, the Commission and the Council regarding the implementation of the Stability and Growth Pact. The European Council endorsed the two Regulations that form part of the Stability and Growth Pact for ensuring budgetary discipline in the EMU. These Regulations also cover the obligations of member states not participating in the euro area. They were subsequently adopted by the Council in July.

3.14 In recognition of the links between a successful and sustainable EMU, the functioning of the internal market and employment, the European Council adopted a separate resolution on Growth and Employment to stress the commitment of member states, the Commission and the Council to keep employment at the top of the political agenda.

3.15 The European Council agreed a Resolution setting out the principles and fundamental elements of a new Exchange Rate Mechanism (ERM2) to be established as from 1 January 1999. The Governors of the Central Banks endorsed the text of this resolution, including the +/- 15 per cent margins.

3.16 The European Council invited the Council and the Commission, in co-operation with the European Monetary Institute, to study effective ways of implementing all provisions of Article 109 of the Treaty. This covers the exchange rate of the euro and international representation of the euro area. The European Council also invited the Council and the Commission to examine and indicate how to improve the processes of economic co-ordination in stage three of EMU consistent with the principles and practices of the Treaty.

3.17 The European Council agreed the texts of the two regulations establishing the legal status of the euro. The regulation under Article 235, concerning the continuity of contracts on the introduction of the single currency, was subsequently adopted at Council. The European Council requested that the regulation under Article 109l(4), concerning the replacement of participating member states' currencies with the euro, including transitional arrangements, be adopted by the Council immediately after the decision on member states' participation in the single currency is taken in the first half of 1998.

3.18 The European Council welcomed and endorsed the choice for the design of the common face of the euro coins.

Broad Economic Guidelines

3.19 In accordance with Article 103(2) of the Treaty, the Amsterdam European Council approved a draft Recommendation for the Broad Guidelines of the Economic Policies of the member states and of the Community. The Council's recommendation sets out the main economic objectives of sustainable non-inflationary and employment creating growth. It covers policies directed at price stability, sound public finances and structural reform. The guidelines will inform the monitoring of economic developments and policies in member states in the context of the multilateral surveillance exercise required under Article 103(3) of the Treaty.

Excessive Deficits

3.20   The 12 May ECOFIN decided to remove the Netherlands and Finland from the list of countries which had an excessive deficit. These two countries together with Denmark, Luxembourg and the Republic of Ireland do not have an excessive deficit. The other ten, including the UK, do. Having established the existence of an excessive deficit, Article 104c.7 of the Treaty provides that the Council shall make recommendations to the member states concerned '... with a view to bringing that situation [the excessive deficit] to an end within a given period'. These recommendations are updated each year and were discussed and for countries other than the UK were agreed in principle at the ECOFIN Council meeting on 12 May. The UK's excessive deficit recommendation was delayed until after the UK's July Budget.

Draft Directive on Cross Border Credit Transfers

3.21   This directive lays down minimum standards for cross-border credit transfer services in the EU.   Following endorsement by the Council and Parliament of the joint text agreed by the Conciliation Committee, the directive was adopted on 27 January. Implementation by member states is to be no later than 14 August 1999.

Draft Directive on Settlement Finality and Collateral Security

3.22   Discussion on the Commission's proposed directive on settlement finality and collateral security continued in a Council Working Group. The aim of the directive is to ensure that payment systems can continue to function in the event of a participant bank failing. The Working Group has agreed certain modifications to the Commission's proposals, the most important being extension of the directive's scope to securities settlement systems.   On 9 June, ECOFIN reviewed progress on the discussions and invited the Working Group to finalise the technical details.

Investor Compensation Directive

3.24   The Investor Compensation Directive (ICD) was adopted on 3 March. The ICD is intended to facilitate the operation of the single market in investment services by setting minimum standards of investor compensation in member states in the event of an investment firm being unable to meet its obligations to investors.

The Directive must be implemented by 26 September 1998.

Amendment to the Capital Adequacy Directive

3.25   On 16 April the European Commission adopted a proposal to amend the Capital Adequacy Directive (CAD). The CAD, which came into force at the beginning of 1996, sets harmonised minimum capital requirements in respect of the securities and investment activities of credit institutions and investment firms passported under the Second Banking Directive and the Investment Services Directive.

3.26   The proposed amending directive will enable credit institutions and investment firms to make use of value-at-risk models for the calculation of market risk capital. Once adopted, it will bring EC legislation in line with the January 1996 amendment to the 1988 Basle Capital Accord (which sets international standards for capital adequacy for international banks).

3.27   The proposal also extends the scope of the CAD to positions in commodities and commodities derivatives. It allows for a transitional period of two years, during which national supervisory authorities may apply a more flexible market risk regime to investment firms with diverse commodity portfolios.

Second Banking Directive

3.28   In June, the Commission issued an interpretative communication setting out its interpretation of two concepts in the Second Banking Directive: freedom to provide services and the general good.

European Investment Bank (EIB): External Lending

3.29   ECOFIN on 27 November 1995 asked the Commission and the EIB to consider jointly a new guarantee arrangement for the Bank in support of its external lending operations. The Commission's report to the Council of 27 June 1996, details of which were set out in the White Paper (paragraph 4.20) covering the period January - June 1996, CM3469, fulfilled that remit. Subsequently, the Commission brought forward proposals for the renewal of the EIB's external lending mandates (for Central and Eastern Europe, Mediterranean, Asia and Latin America, and South Africa) to commence in 1997. Consideration of the proposed new guarantee arrangements was driven largely by a desire by a number of member states to increase the capacity of the EIB to lend. Both issues were the subject of intense negotiations both at official level and in the Council, with the points of dispute being the actual level of the guarantee itself and the amount and regional distribution of the individual mandates. Agreement was finally reached at the ECOFIN meeting on 27 January.

3.30 The main features of the agreement are that:

- The guarantee level has been set at 70 per cent.

- The Mediterranean lending mandate for 1997-99 is 2,310 million ecu (£1,567 million).

- The CEECs mandate is 3,520 million ecu (£2,389 million). In addition, the EIB was invited to come forward with proposals later in the year for a "substantial" pre-accession facility.

- The ALA mandate is 900 million ecu (£611 million).

- The South Africa mandate is 375 million ecu (£254 million).

- Each payment to the Loan Guarantee Fund to be based on the percentage required at payment, target is 15 per cent currently and 14 per cent as soon as is feasible.

Loans to Central and Eastern Europe

3.31 In January 1997, the Council agreed that the second instalment of 100 million ecu (£68 million) of a 200 million ecu (£136 million) loan originally agreed in 1995 for Ukraine could go ahead.

3.32 On 17 March, the Council agreed to reactivate a 70 million ecu (£47 million) loan which had been agreed for Romania in 1994 but which had remained undisbursed.

Harmonisation of the Structures of Excise Duties on Mineral Oils

3.33 A review by the Commission of Directive 92/81 on the harmonisation of the structures of excise duties on mineral oils, required by 31 December 1996, was a precursor to the proposal for a directive restructuring the framework for the taxation of energy products. It concentrated on the derogations that each member state has for internal policy considerations. The review attempted to remove the derogations or impose stricter time limits on their life. A working group of officials eventually reached a compromise on the Commission package and this was adopted by Council on 30 June. Some derogations were set for removal by 31 December 1997 while others have set lifespans and are subject to further review.

Community Framework for the Taxation of Energy Products

3.34   A proposal for a directive restructuring the Community framework for the taxation of energy products (COM(97)30) was introduced at the 17 March ECOFIN. It aims to enhance the existing approximation of national excise duties on mineral oils by increasing minimum rates, and to extend the principle of minimum rates to other energy products, notably solid fuels, natural gas and electricity. It is effectively a successor to earlier proposals for a Community carbon/energy tax, though these also remain on the table for the time being. The Presidency created a High Level Working Group to discuss the proposal, and produced a brief progress report to ECOFIN on 12 May. ECOFIN called on the Commission to do further work on the single market case for the proposal, its environmental and economic justification, and the impact on competitiveness. In the meantime, a lower level official working group met several times to examine technical aspects of the proposal.

Transit Reform

3.35   Community Transit procedures are used for the movement of goods within the Community without payment of the duty and tax payable thereon. The system has been extended to EFTA and some East European countries when it is then known as common transit. Concerned about large scale fraud within the system, the European Parliament set up a Committee of Inquiry into Community Transit. The Committee presented its report in April making a number of recommendations for change. The Commission carried out its own examination of transit and in April published its "Action Plan for Transit in Europe - A New Customs Policy". This sets out the Commission's proposals for procedural and operational changes to Community and common transit taking into account the report of the European Parliament Committee of Inquiry. The Action Plan was presented to the ECOFIN and Internal Market Councils in May and over the following months the Commission will be presenting its detailed legislative proposals for implementing the Plan.

4. Employment, Education and other areas of Community Activity

Employment and Social Affairs Issues

4.1   The 17 April meeting of the Social Affairs Council had a light agenda. The work programme of the Employment and Labour Market Committee was noted. The Presidency observed that there seemed little likelihood of the Council achieving the required unanimity on the draft amendment to the Equal Treatment Directive. There was a further discussion of the Renault closure at Vilvoorde.

Employment and Labour Market Committee.

Following agreement at the December 1996 Social Affairs Council, the Employment and Labour Market Committee held its first meeting in January. Hans Borstlap, the Director General (Employment) of the Netherlands Ministry of Social Affairs and Employment, was elected as the Committee's first Chairman.

The Committee met six times in the first half of 1997. The first Work Programme implemented the Committee's mandates from European Councils, concentrating on debates on labour market performance indicators, benchmarking best practice and non-wage labour costs. The Committee was involved in preparations for the joint employment report to the Amsterdam Council in July. The Committee has set up liaison with the EPC, particularly on the Joint Report and the Broad Economic Guidelines, and with the Social Partners on employment and labour market policy through the Standing Committee on Employment.

The work programme for the remainder of 1997 will continue work on benchmarking, preparations for the Joint Employment report to the Luxembourg Council and the Employment Policy Guidelines. A number of debates on employability and flexibility are scheduled.

4.2   Following agreements on amendments put forward by the UK, a common position was reached on the draft Directive on the Burden of Proof in Sex Discrimination cases; owing to the agreement reached at the Amsterdam European Council, the UK Government was able to take part in discussions. UK amendments were accepted, enabling the Directive to take into account the existing approach of the UK courts in this field. There was discussion of the Davignon Group report on proposals for employee involvement in the

European Company Statute. The Council also agreed Conclusions which note the contribution of the Report.

4.3   Other items on the agenda included: the agreement of a common position on the Chemical Agents Directive and a debate on the future of social protection.

4.4   The Treaty agreed at the Amsterdam European Council included a new Employment Chapter. The new chapter calls for member states and the Community to develop a co-ordinated strategy for employment, and in particular:

- to promote a skilled, trained, adaptable workforce and labour market responsive to economic change.

- to take employment into consideration in the formulation and implementation of Community policies.

- (the Council) to agree a set of employment guidelines each year which member states should take account of in their employment policies.

4.5   The new chapter also provides for the Council to make recommendations to member states on the basis of an annual examination of their employment policies. Article 5 of the new Employment Chapter also gives scope for the funding of employment related incentive measures including exchanges of best practices and pilot projects.

4.6   The European Council called for the European Investment Bank to step up its activities in respect of creating employment by financing high technology projects, intervention in the areas of education, health and environment, and examining the possibility of granting very long term loans for large priority projects.

4.7   The Presidency conclusions on employment , competitiveness and growth called for a special European Council to take place, under the Luxembourg Presidency, to review progress in the implementation of:

- initiatives concerning job creating potentials for small and medium sized enterprises.

- A new Competitiveness Advisory Group.

- The study of good practices on employment policies of member states.

- The initiatives of the European Investment Bank.

Education

4.8   The Council of Education Ministers met in Luxembourg on 26 June and reached agreement on the adoption of a common position on the European Commission proposal to increase the budget of the SOCRATES education programme. The common position will provide for the budget to increase from 850 million ecu (£577 million) over 5 years to 875 million ecu (£594 million). The Council adopted Conclusions on Safety at School, on Information and Communications Technology and Teacher Training, and on the Commission White Paper "Teaching and Learning: Towards the Learning Society". The Council received reports on the Commission's draft Recommendation on Quality Assurance in Higher Education and on the Fifth Research and Development Framework Programme. Ministers also discussed the Commission Green Paper "Education, Training, Research: The Obstacles to Transnational Mobility" and language teaching.

Youth

4.9   No Youth Council was held but the Council's Youth Working Party took forward consideration of the Commission proposal for a European Voluntary Service for Young People.

Health

4.10   The Health Council met on 5 June. The Council noted a working document submitted by the Commission Services on Transmissible Spongiform Encephalopathies and agreed conclusions drawing attention to the need to: continue to keep detailed records of the incidence of Creutzfeldt-Jacob disease and collate and analyse that data at European level; ensure that cases of BSE were reported accurately, including in mainland Europe; and conduct an open debate on food safety policy within the EU, which the Commission has already contributed to in its Green paper on food.

4.11   A common position was agreed on the proposed decision creating a network for the epidemiological surveillance and control of communicable diseases in the European Community, with the Commission reserving its position pending the second reading of the European Parliament.

4.12   A Resolution on the quality and safety of organs and tissues of human origin used for health purposes was agreed, with the Council deciding that a communication should be issued dealing with the following principal points: the legal position within the context of the Treaty regarding cross-border co-operation involving human organs and tissues intended for medical use in the Community; co-operation with international organisations concerned with public health; and current practice in the member states on the traceability of organs and tissues, on quality assurance, and raising public awareness in the Community.

4.13   In relation to the Commission Communication on the present and proposed Community role in combating tobacco consumption, the Council held a policy debate where the member states discussed their positions on the draft Directive on banning tobacco advertising. The UK withdrew its opposition to the draft Directive in principle, but would await the opinion of the Council Legal Services on the appropriate Treaty base for such a Directive before formalising its response.

4.14   The Council heard an oral presentation from Commissioner Flynn, introducing three new proposed health action programmes on: rare diseases, injury prevention and pollution-related diseases.

4.15   A Resolution on the potential problems associated with Doctors moving their practice within the EU was passed. The Commission reserved the right to examine any follow-up action to this Resolution.

The Fourth Framework Programme for Research and Technology Development

4.16   In March, the European Parliament concluded its second reading of Council's common position on the Commission's proposal for 100 million ecu (£68 million) additional funding for the Fourth Framework Programme. The Parliament proposed five amendments, including an increase in the budget. The proposal will now be subject to the conciliation procedure.

The Fifth Framework Programme for Research and Technology Development

4.17   At its meeting on 14-15 May, the Research Council had a substantive debate on the Commission's proposals for the Fifth Framework programme. It was noted that the Commission intended to provide a definitive proposal for the overall budget for the programme in July 1997.

Culture

4.18   Agreement was reached on the "Ariane" programme (Community action programme in the field of literary translation) by the Conciliation Committee on 28 May.

4.19   At the Conciliation Committee meeting on 28 May, there was no agreement between the Council and the European Parliament on the text of the proposed "Raphael" (Community action programme in the field of cultural heritage) programme. Agreement was subsequently reached at a second meeting on 2 July.

4.20   On 19 June, the Council adopted a Directive amending the 1989 Broadcasting Directive (the "TV without Frontiers" Directive).

4.21   At the Culture Council on 30 June, Ministers agreed draft Decisions on the future of European cultural action, and on cross-border fixed book prices in European linguistic areas.

4.22   The Culture Council also discussed the future of the European Cities of Culture initiative; the Commission's proposal for a European Audiovisual Guarantee Fund; and the Commission's Green Paper on the protection of minors and human dignity in audiovisual and information services.

Tourism

4.23   The Council was unable to agree a decision on a multiannual programme to assist European Tourism "Philoxenia". The Presidency produced a revised compromise proposal, which takes account of the concerns of member states expressed previously and which it hopes will result in a Council decision this year.

5. External Relations, including Trade and Aid

Enlargement

5.1   Acting on the pre-accession strategy agreed in December 1994 at the Essen European Council, EU ministers met their Central European counterparts to continue discussion of issues across the three pillars. Meetings were held by ministers in the areas of economic and finance, environment, the internal market, agriculture, foreign affairs, research and development, energy and justice and home affairs.

5.2   The Amsterdam European Council of 16-17 June looked forward to the European Commission's presentation of the Agenda 2000 communication which was expected to include the Opinions on the Central European applicants. These were subsequently delivered on 16 July. The Council Conclusions invited the General Affairs Council to present a comprehensive report to the European Council at its December meeting in Luxembourg where the necessary decisions on the overall enlargement process would be taken. These would include the practical arrangements for the initial phase of negotiations and the reinforcement of the Union's pre-accession strategy.

5.3   Association Councils with Cyprus and Turkey were held on 25 February and 29 April, respectively.

World Trade Organisation (WTO)

In February and March respectively, WTO negotiations on liberalising trade in basic telecommunications services and information technology were successfully concluded. Together, the Agreements provide for tariff reductions on about one trillion dollars worth of global trade in goods and services. Further negotiations on market opening measures in the financial services sector began in April; the deadline for conclusion is 12 December 1997.

The Singapore WTO Ministerial in December 1996 agreed an Action Plan to help integrate least developed countries into the world trading system. One of its objectives is a multilateral commitment to duty free access for exports from these countries. The EU has agreed to increase market access for the poorest countries which are not covered by the Lomé Agreement. A High Level Meeting took place in October this year to look at how best to coordinate the provision of technical assistance on trade matters for the least developed.

There is now provision in the WTO's new work programme for UK priorities for tackling trade barriers, for example on further trade facilitation, government procurement and on technical product standards.

Preferential Trade Agreements

5.4   In April of this year the Council agreed conclusions on the development of the EU's trade policy and its preferential trade agreements. These established a framework within which any future proposals for EU/third party preferential agreements should be considered. The Amsterdam European Council took note of the conclusions.

Former Yugoslavia

5.5   The General Affairs Council on 29 April agreed to extend trade preferences to the Federal Republic of Yugoslavia (Serbia and Montenegro). The preferences are subject to renewal by the end of 1997. The Council will decide whether or not to renew preferential access on the basis of its assessment of the progress made by the government of the Federal Republic of Yugoslavia towards democratisation and a free media.

5.6   The 29 April General Affairs Council also agreed conclusions on the development of contractual relations between the Community and Croatia, the Federal Republic of Yugoslavia, Bosnia Herzegovina, the Former Yugoslav Republic of Macedonia and Albania. As part of this process, the Community signed a Trade and Co-operation Agreement and a Transport Agreement with the Former Yugoslav Republic of Macedonia.

Central Asia

5.7   The EU continued to provide the countries of Eastern Europe and Central Asia with technical assistance under the TACIS programme to assist the process of reform.

5.8   A Partnership and Co-operation Agreement was initialled with Turkmenistan on 24 May. Protocols to the Partnership and Co-operation Agreements with Ukraine, Moldova and Russia were signed (on 10 April, 15 May and 21 May respectively) to enable the new member states (Austria, Sweden and Finland) to become parties to these Agreements.

5.9   An EU/Russia Summit took place in Moscow on 3 March.

Mediterranean

5.10   An Interim Association Agreement with the PLO on behalf of the Palestinian Authority was signed on 24 February.

5.11   The second Euro-Mediterranean Foreign Ministers meeting was held in Valletta, Malta on 15-16 April. It reviewed progress to date and agreed priorities for future action.

5.12   The UK held a Euro-Mediterranean Investment Conference in London on 6-7 March. This promoted liberalisation of the Mediterranean economies and EU investment in the region. The Conference was used to launch Investor Guides prepared following detailed contacts with governments and the private sector in the Mediterranean.

EU/US

EU/US Summits are held every six months under the New Transatlantic Agenda, signed in December 1995. The Presidency and the Commission represent the EU. The latest Summit was held on 28 May in The Hague. Key agreements were reached on customs co-operation and chemical precursors. There was also detailed discussion on other topics of mutual interest, including Iran, China, drugs and international crime, and the Middle East Peace Process. Business from both sides of the Atlantic have continued to be actively involved in the Transatlantic Business Dialogue, as a result of which, the EU and US have signed a Mutual Recognition Agreement which removed the need for duplicating standards testing of products such as pharmaceuticals and telecommunications equipment which will facilitate transatlantic trade. Tensions continue over the US use of extraterritorial sanctions, and the EU is in dialogue with the US in an attempt to resolve these issues.

EU/Canada

5.13   An EU/Canada Summit was held in Denver on 20 June. The Presidency and Commission represented the EU. The Summit reviewed progress on the EU/Canada Action Plan and Political Declaration, signed in December 1996. Prior to the Summit, the EU concluded with Canada Agreements on Customs Co-operation, Mutual Recognition of Standards and on Veterinary Equivalence (see paragraph 7.13), as well as agreeing the terms of reference for a joint study on removing barriers to EU/Canada trade.

EU/Japan

5.14   The sixth EU/Japan Summit was held in The Hague on 25 June. The usual economic dialogue was expanded to cover political matters. Both sides agreed on the need for a successful ASEM (Asia Europe Meeting) Summit to be held in London in April 1998 while, on economic issues, Japan confirmed that broad-based deregulation remained an essential part of its structural reform programme.

EU/Australia

5.15   On 26 June, the EU and Australia signed a Joint Declaration which provides the foundation for the further strengthening of their relations. Although non-binding, the Declaration covers all areas of

EU business and underlines the importance of EU/Australia co-operation.

EU/Hong Kong

In April the Commission issued a Communication on the *European Union and Hong Kong Beyond 1997*. This sets out the range of shared interests and close ties between the EU and Hong Kong and suggests how EU/Hong Kong relations should develop after the handover. The Communication highlights the importance of maintaining Hong Kong's distinct international role and autonomy and suggests the Community should do more to encourage the development of ties and to put trade and economic co-operation with Hong Kong on a more permanent footing. The General Affairs Council on 2 June endorsed the thrust of the Communication and underscored the broad political message of EU support for the Hong Kong Special Administrative Region (HKSAR). The 16-17 June European Council in Amsterdam subsequently emphasised the importance the EU attaches to full respect for the rights and freedoms of the Hong Kong people and the high degree of autonomy accorded to Hong Kong under the Sino-British Joint Declaration and the Basic Law of the HKSAR.

EU/ASEAN

5.16   The 12th EU/ASEAN (Association of South East Asian Nations) Ministerial meeting was held in Singapore on 13-14 February. The meeting launched a "new dynamic" in EU/ASEAN relations, setting the agenda for closer political, economic and development co-operation between the EU and ASEAN. At Singapore, Vietnam formally acceded to the 1980 EC/Vietnam Co-operation Agreement.

ASEM

5.17   The first ASEM (Asia Europe Meeting) Foreign Ministers meeting took place in Singapore on 14-15 February. It reviewed follow-up work to and initiatives since the 1996 ASEM Summit in Bangkok as well as agreeing proposals for future co-operation between the two regions. The UK will host the next ASEM Summit in London in April 1998.

Gulf

5.18   Ministers from the EU and the Gulf Co-operation Council (Saudi Arabia, Kuwait, Qatar, United Arab Emirates, Bahrain and Oman) met at the EC/GCC Joint Co-operation Council in Doha, Qatar on 17 February.

Latin America

5.19   The EU/Central America Ministerial meeting (San Jose XIII) was held in The Hague, Netherlands on 25-26 February. The EU was represented by the Troika (Ireland, Netherlands, Luxembourg). The seventh Institutionalised Ministerial meeting between the EU and the Rio Group was held in Noordwijk on 7-8 April.

5.20   The EU/Mercosur Sub-Committee on Trade met in Brussels on 26 May; the EC/Uruguay Joint Committee met in Montevideo on 30 May; the EC/Paraguay Joint Committee met in Asuncion on 2 June; the EC/Chile Sub-Committee on Trade met in Brussels on 12 June; and the EU/Central America Sub-Committee on Trade met in Panama on 19 June.

Asia-Pacific

5.21   The EC/India Joint Commission met in New Delhi on 12-13 May; the EC/Sri Lanka Joint Committee met in Colombia on 15 May.

5.22   Signature of the EC/Cambodia and EC/Laos Co-operation Agreements took place in Luxembourg on 29 April.

South Africa

5.23   Negotiations on the establishment of a Free Trade Area with the Republic of South Africa continued. South Africa acceded to partial membership of the Lomé Convention at the ACP-EC Council in April.

Relations with Developing Countries

5.24   The UK ratified the Mid-Term Review of the fourth ACP-EC Convention of Lomé on 21 May. The Mid-Term Review will come into force when two-thirds of the ACP (African, Caribbean and Pacific countries) and all EU member states have ratified it. Initial discussions on a successor to the fourth Lomé Convention continued, on the basis of a Commission Green Paper, at an informal ACP-EU ministerial meeting in Maastricht in April. The future of Lomé was also one of the subjects considered at the annual ACP-EC Council held in Luxembourg in April.

5.25   The Development Council of 5 June adopted a common position on a draft Regulation covering NGO co-financing. The Regulation sets out a legal framework for EC expenditure, and will give member states closer control over aid expenditure and facilitate objective evaluation. Three Resolutions were also agreed, one establishing institutional mechanisms to improve coherence between development and other EC policies; one setting out plans to create a more coherent strategic framework for research activities in developing countries; and one on the evaluation of the food aid programme. The Council also adopted three sets of Conclusions, on the needs of indigenous peoples in EC development programmes, on the extension of a pilot exercise in operational coordination to all developing countries, and on the Court of Auditors report concerning EU Humanitarian Aid.

6. The Single Market

6.1   The 13 March Internal Market Council (IMC) reached political agreement with a view to a common position on a draft directive on the legal protection of designs, and common positions on a draft directive relating to the maximum design speed of wheeled agricultural or forestry tractors and a draft directive amending a Directive on dietary foods. The Commission made oral presentations of their Green Paper on public procurement in the European Union (Exploring the Way Forward) and their Communication: Follow-up to the Green Paper on Copyright and Related Rights in the Information Society. There was also a joint meeting with the Associated Countries where the Commission presented its report on the first year of operation of the Technical Assistance Information Exchange Office (TAIEX).

Action Plan for the Single Market

The 13 March IMC debated the Commission's proposed Action Plan for the Single Market. The Council requested that the Commission elaborate its ideas for the plan so that further discussion could take place. The Commission formally presented the Action Plan to the 21 May IMC, where there was broad agreement for the Plan and its four 'Strategic Targets'. The final Plan was welcomed by the Amsterdam European Council, which endorsed the overall objective and the four Strategic Targets as a basis for realising the full potential of the Single Market.

The four Strategic Targets in the Action Plan are:

- Making the rules more effective.
- Dealing with key market distortions.
- Removing sectoral obstacles to market integration.
- Delivering a Single Market for the benefit of all citizens.

The Plan focuses on the transposition into national law and effective enforcement of existing legislation, as well as simplification and improvement of rules in some key areas, such as public procurement and the mutual recognition of national arrangements. Amongst the legislative elements of the Plan, there is commitment to liberalisation of financial services, telecommunications and energy markets, and measures dealing with new technologies such as biotechnology and electronic commerce.

6.2   The 21 May IMC reached common positions on a draft directive to facilitate practice of the profession of lawyers on a permanent basis in a member state other than that in which the qualification was obtained and on a draft directive concerning foods and food ingredients treated with ionizing radiation. A political agreement to a common position was reached on a draft directive on in vitro diagnostic medical devices. The Commission made presentations on the action plan for customs transit in Europe, on the outcome of the proceedings of the working party chaired by Viscount Davignon concerning a Statute for a European Company, and on the Commission Communication on a European Initiative in Electronic Commerce.

7.   Agriculture, Fisheries and Food

AGRICULTURE

1997/98 CAP Price Fixing

7.1   At the Agriculture Council on 23-25 June, agreement was reached on the Commission's annual price proposals. The main price fixing package for the 1997/98 marketing year was agreed within budgetary guidelines. The key points of the agreed package are described in more detail in the Annex to this Chapter.

Bovine Spongiform Encephalopathy (BSE)

7.2   The Government continued to implement measures designed to eradicate BSE and protect public health in the UK, and to fulfil the conditions laid down in the Florence Agreement with the aim of securing a progressive resumption in the export of beef and beef products. Progress on these preconditions was as follows:

- Significant progress had been made in the **implementation of the selective slaughter programme**. Northern Ireland had all but completed its cull of animals born in the province and in Great Britain 37 per cent natal herds identified in the selective slaughter programme had been visited by the State Veterinary Service (SVS).

- **Introduction of an effective animal identification and movement recording system**. A total of 2,365,815 cattle passports had been issued for cattle born or imported after 1 July 1996. A computerised cattle traceability system is being developed and will be in place during 1998, well before the Commission's deadline of late 1999 (see snapshot essay).

- **Legislation for the removal of mammalian meat and bone meal from feed mills and farms**. The Commission inspected the arrangements in respect of animal feed and mammalian meat and bone meal on 26 - 29 July 1996 and confirmed that it was content. That position was confirmed in discussion with the Standing Veterinary Committee on 10-11 September. The arrangements were inspected again on 9-13 June and were found to be satisfactory.

- **Effective implementation of the Over Thirty Month Scheme (OTMS).** Over 1,600,000 animals had been culled under the OTMS since March 1996.

- Controls on slaughterhouses to ensure **the removal of Specified Bovine Material (SBM)** had been strengthened and tightened. The monthly Enforcement Bulletins continued to show sustained improvement in ensuring compliance with SBM controls; there had been no instances of spinal cord not being removed in licensed slaughterhouses in Great Britain for the previous fifteen months. There has been one finding of a small piece of spinal cord in a slaughterhouse in Northern Ireland.

7.3   The Government submitted revised proposals for the Export Certified Herds Scheme in the light of the Scientific Veterinary Committee's opinion. The Government has also had preliminary discussions with the Commission about proposals for an export scheme for meat from animals born after 1 August 1996.

7.4   In June, evidence began to emerge of a suspected fraud involving the illegal export of UK beef to third countries via at least two other member states. The suspicions are subject to a full investigation in conjunction with the Commission's anti-fraud unit and enforcement authorities in other member states.

7.5   The European Parliament's (EP) Temporary Committee of Inquiry (TCI) to investigate alleged contraventions in the implementation of Community Law in relation to BSE, published its final report on 6 February. The report was highly critical of both the Commission and the UK Government's handling of the BSE situation. The EP adopted a compromise resolution on the TCI's report on 19 February, endorsing the report and urging implementation of its recommendations, the main one of which is a conditional motion of censure on the Commission if it fails to take appropriate action in light of the criticisms and recommendations made by the TCI.

7.6   On 23-24 April, the EP set up a new Temporary Committee (EPTC) to monitor the Commission's follow up actions to the TCI's recommendations, a number of which concern the UK. In particular, the TCI recommended that legal action be taken against the UK for the previous Minister's decision not to give evidence to the TCI and that the Commission extract compensation from the UK for costs to the EC as a whole arising from the BSE crisis. The Commission has advised the EPTC that neither recommendation could be sustained as a legal challenge.

Beef Traceability and Labelling

On 21-22 April the Agriculture Council agreed major changes to the system for identifying cattle in Europe and also established rules for labelling beef when claims are made about the origin or quality of the meat.

These changes followed the BSE crisis. They are intended to meet the concern of consumers that cattle, and meat derived from them, should be more easily traceable. In future, cattle will have to have two eartags, each eartag recording the unique identification code of the animal, and passports recording all the farms they have been on. In addition, there will be computerised systems which hold information on cattle registrations and movements. These computerised databases must be fully established by 1 January 2000. To meet this obligation for a cattle passport system the registration database in Great Britain is being enhanced in 1998 to include cattle movement data. A registration and movement database has already been established in Northern Ireland. Finally, farmers will continue to have to keep on-farm registers for their cattle, as they do at present.

All this will mean that it will be much easier than it has been in the past to trace cattle from the farm of birth through to the slaughterhouse.

The new rules on labelling mean that where claims are made at the retail stage about the origin of beef (or about feeding practices used or maturation processes), consumers can be reassured that the information is verifiable. Giving information on the origin of beef is not however obligatory, at least until 2000.

The UK supported these changes, and voted in favour of them in the Agriculture Council. But in the original form in which they were put forward by the Commission, they would have been over-bureaucratic and, in some areas, unworkable. For example, the original Commission proposal on cattle identification appeared to require cattle which already had eartags to be given new ones; this would have been impossible to enforce and would have led to major animal welfare problems. On labelling, the Commission wanted their proposals to extend to meat products such as pies and pasties; this would have created real difficulties for the meat products industry and, if workable at all, would have led to markedly increased costs for both industry and consumers. Pressure from the UK led to significant improvements in the new rules.

Revision of Health Conditions for Intra-Community Trade in Cattle and Pigs

7.7   Council Directive 64/432/EEC laying down animal health rules for intra-community trade in cattle and pigs has been amended on over 40 occasions. Council Directive 97/12/EC consolidating and updating Directive 64/432/EEC was adopted at the 18-19 March Agriculture Council. The amended Directive comes into force on 1 July 1998. The Commission is committed to review and put forward proposals for amendments to the annexes, for adoption before 1 July 1998. There is also a requirement for a computer database recording cattle and pig movements to be in operation in each member state from 31 December 1999.

Inter-Governmental Conference - Sentient Beings

7.8   Agreement was reached at the Amsterdam European Council on a Protocol to the draft Treaty of Amsterdam, recognising that animals are sentient beings and requiring their welfare needs to be properly taken into account in the development of the Community's policies on agriculture, transport, the internal market and research.

Apiculture

7.9   The Agriculture Council on 23-25 June adopted the Commission proposal for a regulation to improve the production and marketing of honey. The main aim of Regulation 1221/97 is to assist the beekeeping sector in dealing with the burden of the bee disease varroa. It seeks to achieve this by providing for EU reimbursement of up to 50 per cent of member states' expenditure on certain measures to protect bee health and to improve honey production. The Commission is now preparing detailed rules to implement the regulation.

World Trade Organisation (WTO): Agricultural Issues

7.10   WTO member countries agreed in December 1996 to undertake a process of analysis and information exchange in the lead-up to the next multilateral negotiations on agricultural trade liberalisation, due to begin at the turn of the century.   The process, which is intended to allow countries to understand the issues and identify their interests, has now begun in the form of informal meetings of the WTO's Agriculture Committee.

Agricultural Trade Disputes:

(i)   Hormones Ban

7.11   The United States and Canada initiated WTO dispute proceedings in 1996 against the EU's ban on the use of certain growth-promoting hormones and on the import of meat from hormone-treated animals. The UK opposed the ban when it was introduced, on the grounds that it was not scientifically justified. In May the dispute Panels produced their interim reports. Although the reports were confidential to the parties to the disputes, it was widely reported that they found the EU to have breached the WTO Agreement on Sanitary and Phytosanitary Measures.

(ii)   Bananas

7.12   In April 1996 the US, Guatemala, Honduras, Mexico and Ecuador requested the establishment of a WTO Dispute Settlements Panel on the EC banana regime, which they claimed discriminated unfairly against their own traders or producers. The Panel's final report, which was circulated to WTO Members on 22 May, found that several key features of the EU regime were incompatible with the GATT, the General Agreement on Trade and Services (GATS) and the Import Licensing Agreement and that most of these infringements were not covered by the WTO Waiver for preferential treatment of imports from African, Caribbean and Pacific (ACP) countries required by the Lomé Convention. The EU lodged an appeal with the WTO Appellate Body on 11 June.

Veterinary Equivalence Negotiations

7.13   The Commission has been negotiating agreements with third countries for mutual recognition of veterinary standards. Technical agreement was reached with the USA in April (excluding poultry meat) although the Council's approval has yet to be obtained. Agreements are also being negotiated with Argentina, Australia, Bulgaria, Canada (see paragraph 5.13), Chile, the Czech Republic, Hungary, Poland, Romania, the Slovak Republic, Switzerland and Uruguay.

Oilseeds

7.14   The Agriculture Council in October 1996 had previously agreed in principle that the advance oilseed payment should be deferred until 16 October 1997 thereby freeing funds in the 1997 budget year to meet anticipated expenditure on additional beef measures. However, no final decision on this (or the associated reductions in aid for arable crops and set-aside) was made as part of the 1997 price-fixing.

Flax

7.15   On 20 January, the Agriculture Council agreed to tighten up the rules of the flax regime. This included a requirement for obligatory contracts between growers and approved processors, tightening up of checks including cross-checking against the Integrated Administration and Control System (IACS), and provision for laying down criteria for normal cultivation, in particular by setting minimum yields to be respected.

Tobacco

7.16   The Commission presented a paper on options for reform of the tobacco regime to the 20-21 January Agriculture Council and the European Parliament. The 17-18 February Agriculture Council asked the Commission to produce formal reform proposals once the European Parliament had given its opinion on the options paper.

Olive Oil

7.17   The Commission presented a paper on options for reform of the olive oil regime to the 17-18 February Agriculture Council and the European Parliament. The 19-20 May Agriculture Council asked the Commission to produce formal reform proposals once the European Parliament has given its opinion on the options paper.

Arable Area Payments

7.18   Modifications were agreed to Council Regulation 1765/92 which is the basic regulation for Arable Area Payments. These give greater flexibility to member states in applying penalties when regional base areas are exceeded. Member states wishing to take advantage of this facility are required to notify the Commission of their proposed arrangements by 15 May each year although for 1997/98 this will be 15 September. In addition, penalties can be waived by the Commission where the base area has been exceeded due to exceptional climatic conditions.

Operation of the Agrimonetary System

7.19   Following the strengthening of the pound sterling, the Irish punt and the Italian lira in late 1996/early 1997, on 18-19 March the Agriculture Council adopted Regulation 724/97, extending until January 1999 the temporary rules on agrimonetary compensation. These were previously agreed at the June 1995 Agriculture Council for all member states whose agricultural conversion rates undergo appreciable revaluations, as a result of currency appreciation, before the end of April 1998. The rules freeze until 1 January 1999 the agricultural conversion rates (green rates) used to convert CAP direct payments to farmers into national currencies, so that they are protected from the effects of revaluations of the agricultural conversion rate.

7.20   The UK underwent three appreciable revaluations of its agricultural conversion rates in the first half of 1997 (21 January, 29 March and 5 June). It was, however, identified that the freezing of these rates could lead to the persistence of large green rate/market rate gaps at the start of the Third Stage of EMU. On 19 March the Agriculture Council, therefore, agreed to limit the freeze in the green rate for direct payments: the frozen rate is allowed to exceed the green rate applied to other schemes by no more than 11.5%. The limit applies equally to all member states that have experienced appreciable revaluations, and to all those that do so before the end of April 1998.

7.21   The decision by the Agriculture Council on 17-19 March also established the principle of compensation (up to 50% EU funded) to offset the income effects of revaluations for CAP payments not covered by the green rate freeze. The Council devolved to the Commission responsibility for setting the maximum aid available, using a precisely defined formula for assessing income loss in the sectors where CAP supports play a significant role in the market. The Council also agreed that an automatic review of the need for the aid should take place six months after a revaluation (reduced to three months for successive revaluations), which can lead to the adjustment of the compensation to take account of any subsequent devaluations during that period.

FISHERIES

Internal Regime

7.22   On 15 April, the Fisheries Council reached agreement on the fourth Multiannual Guidance Programme (MAGP IV) for restructuring the Community's fishing sector during the period 1997-2001. The Programme aims to bring fishing effort into better balance with available fish stocks by requiring reductions of up to 30 per cent in fishing effort for the most depleted stocks. On 15 April, the Fisheries Council also reached agreement on the allocation between member states of the Total Allowable Catch for Atlanto-Scandian herring.

7.23   On 28 April, the Council adopted a decision allowing the Italian Government to re-allocate structural funds already granted to provide incentives to encourage Italian fishermen to diversify away from drift net fishing in the Mediterranean.

External Regime

7.24   Protocols were initialled during the period renewing the EU's fisheries agreements with Equatorial Guinea, Guinea Bissau, Ivory Coast and Senegal. Protocols were also signed to amend certain provisions of the current EU/Mauritania fisheries agreement and to set out the conditions for joint enterprises under the current EU/Latvia agreement.

FOOD

Changes in DGXXIV

7.25   In response to the EP's TCI report on BSE, the President of the Commission announced his intention to reorganise the way in which the Commission obtains and uses scientific advice on food safety and consumer health, and the way in which it operates its food, veterinary and phytosanitary control and inspection services. It is the Commission's declared intention to place food safety and consumer health at the core of food policy and to create a clearer separation between responsibility for legislation and responsibility for scientific advice and inspections.

7.26   Directorate General XXIV has been reorganised under the Commissioner for Consumer Policy and Health Protection to take responsibility for relevant Scientific Committees, the newly enlarged Food and Veterinary Office (FVO), and a new unit dealing with the assessment of consumer health risks. The FVO will undertake the food hygiene, veterinary and plant health inspection and control responsibilities of the Commission with the overall objective of providing a harmonised control and inspection covering all parts of the food production chain.

Food Additives

7.27   European Parliament and Council Directive 96/83/EC of 19 December 1996 amending Directive 94/35/EC on sweeteners for use in foodstuffs was implemented in the UK by the Sweeteners in Food (Amendment) Regulations 1997 and came into force on 14 April. Parallel legislation was introduced in Northern Ireland.

Novel Foods and Novel Food Ingredients

7.28   Following agreement in conciliation, the Novel Foods Regulation, which requires pre-market safety assessment for all novel foods, including foods consisting of, containing or obtained from genetically modified organisms, was adopted on 27 January and came into force on 15 May.   Related UK legislation on fees and penalties came into force on 16 June.

Annex to Chapter 7

The Common Agricultural Policy (CAP) Price Settlement for 1997/98 and Related Measures

Cereals and Rice

1.   *For 1997/98, the Council agreed a reduction from 1.1 ecu/tonne to 1 ecu/tonne in the monthly increments in the cereals intervention price. For rice the monthly increments on intervention price were reduced from 2.28 ecu/tonne to 2 ecu/tonne.*

Sugar

2.   *Monthly storage refund payments were reduced from 0.42 ecu/100kg to 0.38 ecu/100kg.*

Olive Oil

3.   *With the exception of the intervention price (which was reduced to 180.58 ecu/100kg) the institutional prices and aid rates were maintained at last year's level. The deduction from consumption aid to finance trade organisations expenses in administering the aid was increased from 5.5% to 8%.*

Grain Legumes

4.   *No changes were made and the aid rates were maintained at last year's level.*

Textile fibres

5.   *For silkworms and cotton, there was no change in prices. For fibre flax, the amount to be paid to beneficiaries was fixed at 815.86 ecu/ha. Funding for promotional purposes was reduced to zero. The aid rate for hemp was reduced from 865.48 ecu/ha to 716.63 ecu/ha.*

Wine

6.   *The Council accepted a Commission proposal to retain broadly the status quo, pending major reform of the wine regime.*

Tobacco

7.   *Rollover of guarantee thresholds and premia, pending presentation of review proposals.*

Pigmeat

8.   The basic price for pigmeat of the standard quality remained unchanged at 1509 ecu/tonne.

Dried Fodder, Protein Crops and Linseed, Oilseeds, Fruit and Vegetables, Seeds, Milk, Beef and Veal, Sheep and Goatmeat

9.   No changes were made and the aid rates were maintained at last year's level.

Related Issues

10.   The set-aside rate for 1998/99 was fixed at 5 per cent and the penalty set-aside suspended for that year. As regards arable area payments, the Agriculture Council is to address the problems of overcompensation of arable farmers in forthcoming discussions on reform of the arable regime. The Council also invited the Commission to submit proposals enabling member states to make arable area payments conditional on the respect of environmental provisions.

8. Environment

Auto-Oil - Stage 1

8.1   On 3 March, the Environment Council discussed the two directives on proposed fuel quality and car emission standards by 2000 (Auto-Oil Stage 1). It was agreed that the Commission should bring forward their proposals for mandatory fuel and car emissions for 2005 by the end of 1998. On 19-20 June, the Environment Council agreed a common position on these two directives.

Environmental Impact Assessment

8.2   The Environment Council adopted a Directive amending Directive 85/337 on the assessment of the effects of certain public and private projects on the environment on 3 March. This Directive is regarded as one of the main Community instruments for preventing environmental damage at source.

Funding of Non-Governmental Organisations (NGOs)

8.3   On 3 March, the Environment Council agreed a common position on the Decision on a Community action programme promoting NGOs primarily active in the field of environmental protection. The general objective of this programme is to promote the activities of the NGOs at a European level by contributing to the development and implementation of Community environmental policy and legislation.

Emissions of Volatile Organic Compounds

8.4   On 3 March, the Commission presented to the Environment Council its recently adopted proposals for a directive on the emission of volatile organic compounds (VOCs) from industrial and commercial installations. The directive aims to reduce Europe-wide emissions of VOCs by 50 per cent. The Environment Council reached political agreement on the proposal on 19-20 June. A common position is likely to be agreed during the Luxembourg Presidency.

Implementing Community Environmental Law

8.5   The draft Council resolution on the drafting, implementation and enforcement of Community Environmental Law was discussed by the Environment Council on 3 March. The objective of the resolution is to improve the effectiveness of Community environmental legislation by ensuring that it is fully implemented and enforced by member states. The resolution was agreed at the Environment Council on 19-20 June.

Climate Change

8.6   On 3 March, the Environment Council agreed conclusions which established the Community's negotiating position for the preparatory meetings for the Third Conference of the Parties to the Framework Convention on Climate Change to be held in Kyoto in December of this year. The Convention aims to reduce greenhouse gas emissions. On 19-20 June, the Environment Council agreed conclusions which will further develop the Community's negotiating position, with a negotiating target of at least a 7.5 per cent reduction by 2005.

Leghold Traps

8.7   On 3 March, the Environment Council discussed the position of negotiations on a proposed Council decision concerning the signing and conclusion of an international agreement between the European Community, Canada and the Russian Federation on humane trapping standards. On 19-20 June, the Environment Council could not, however, reach agreement on the proposal to endorse the agreement. The Presidency therefore decided that a decision on the agreement should be postponed.

Water Framework Directive

8.8   The Commission presented to the Environment Council its proposals for a Water Framework Directive on 3 March. The directive would require member states to draw up programmes for achieving good quality rivers, lakes and other waters by 2010. On 19-20 June, the Environment Council held an orientation debate on the directive. It received support from most member states, although greater definition of the objectives to be achieved is needed.

Environmental Agreements

8.9   On 3 March, the Environment Council discussed the use of Environment Agreements. The Agreements are being concluded on a voluntary basis mainly at national level between governments and industries in order to enhance environmental protection. On 19-20 June, the Environment Council agreed conclusions on Environmental Agreements.

Environmental Taxes

8.10   The Commission made a presentation on a communication on environmental taxes and charges on 3 March. The main objective of the communication is to clarify legal issues in relation to the use of environmental taxes and charges by member states in order to ensure their compatibility with Community law, without distorting the single market.

Montreal Protocol

8.11   The negotiating directives for the 9th meeting of the Parties to the Montreal Protocol, to be held in Montreal on 15-17 September, were discussed by the Environment Council on 19-20 June. The Protocol, which aims to protect the ozone layer, has been successively tightened up over its ten year history. This year, the focus is on the phase out date for methyl bromide, a widely used agricultural fumigant which damages the ozone layer.

Acidification

8.12   The Environment Council held an orientation debate on the Community strategy to combat acidification on 19-20 June. The strategy aims to substantially reduce emissions in order to combat acid rain. Although some Northern European member states strongly supported the strategy, other delegations expressed doubts.

UNGASS

8.13   On 19-20 of June, the Environment Council agreed Conclusions on the United Nations General Assembly Special Sessions (UNGASS). The Special Session is a 5 year review since the Rio Earth Summit.

9. Transport

Road

9.1   On 11 March, the Transport Council debated proposals for the introduction of a new digital tachograph. On 17-18 June the Council reached political agreement on a draft Regulation which will require new commercial vehicles to be fitted with electronic tachographs when such instruments have been type approved.

9.2   The Transport Council debated on 11 March, and again on 17-18 June, without reaching a conclusion, a draft directive on the taxation of heavy goods vehicles, and on the conditions on which member states may toll or charge such vehicles for the use of their motorways.

9.3   Also on 11 March, the Transport Council agreed a Resolution calling on member states which are introducing new electronic fee collection systems for road pricing to use the technical standards developed by CEN (the European standardisation body).

9.4   On 17-18 June, the Transport Council debated road safety, and agreed conclusions which, in particular, encouraged the Commission to take forward ideas on exchange of best practice. Conclusions were also agreed endorsing a Commission report on road transport telematics and inviting further work in this area. Also at the Transport Council on 17-18 June, the Commission undertook to report by the end of the year, with any proposals on the growth of weekend and holiday lorry restrictions.

Rail

9.5   At the Transport Council on 11 March, the Commission gave a report on trans-European rail freight freeways, the aim of which is to encourage the transfer of freight from road to rail by allowing greater freedom of access by train operators to the Community's rail network. On 17-18 June, the Transport Council agreed conclusions welcoming the Commission communication.

9.6   On 11 March, the Transport Council reached political agreement on a draft Regulation to continue community funding for combined transport projects aimed at encouraging the transfer of traffic from road to more environmentally friendly modes of transport.

Sea

9.7   On 17-18 June, the Transport Council reached political agreement on a Directive requiring counting of passengers on all sea voyages and the registration of the name, gender and other details of passengers on voyages over 20 miles, subject to certain exemptions and derogations. Political agreement was also reached at the same Council on a Directive bringing Community rules on seafarer training into line with the 1995 revision of the International Maritime Organisation (IMO) Convention on Standards of Training, Certification and Watchkeeping for Seafarers.

9.8   Also on 17-18 June, the Transport Council debated a Commission communication on maritime external relations, and agreed conclusions welcoming a Commission report on short sea shipping.

Air

9.9   On 11 March, the Transport Council reached political agreement on an amendment to Directive 92/14 on aircraft noise. Its main effect is to update the list of aircraft from developing nations exempted until 2002 from the phase-out of some noisier aircraft.

9.10   Also on 11 March, the Transport Council agreed terms of reference for a high level group of officials to consider possible Community involvement in the European Organisation for the Safety of Air Navigation (EUROCONTROL), which co-ordinates air traffic management arrangements within Europe, and in a European aviation safety authority (EASA). On 17-18 June, the Transport Council agreed conclusions on Community involvement in EUROCONTROL and on work towards the creation of a new EASA.

9.11   On 11 March, the Transport Council was invited to comment on a draft resolution, to be considered further by the ECOFIN Council, for a Commission study into the economic and environmental effects of ending the exemption from duty for the fuel used in international aviation. The Resolution was adopted by the ECOFIN Council in June.

9.12   On 17-18 June, the Transport Council reached political agreement on a Directive to co-ordinate and improve members states' arrangements for the safety inspection of third country aircraft using EU airports.

9.13   Also raised at the Transport Council on 17-18 June were the Community's aviation negotiations with the US and with ten countries of Central and Eastern Europe, the latter being aimed at extending the aviation single market to those countries.

General

9.14   On 11 March, the Transport Council broadly endorsed a report from the Commission on proposals aimed at taking forward the Community's negotiations with Switzerland on road and air transport agreements.

9.15   On 11 March, the Council agreed a common position on a draft Directive to continue for another four years the present arrangements harmonising the start and end dates of summer time throughout the Community. The Council and Commission agreed a joint declaration on the need for a study of the effects of summer time.

10. Industry and Energy Issues

EC Merger Regulation (ECMR)

10.1   Council Regulation No 1310/97 amending the EC Merger Regulation No 4064/89 on the control of concentrations between undertakings was adopted on 30 June and comes into force on 1 March 1998. Mergers with a Community dimension are subject to examination by the Commission. The main changes are: introduction of a mechanism to transfer certain transitional mergers to the Commission's "one-stop shop"; incorporation of all "full-function" joint ventures into the ECMR; and provision for a further threshold review by 1 July 2000.

Energy Policy

10.2   In response to requests from member states, the Commission issued a document in April entitled "An Overall View on Energy Policy and Actions" and is the first stage of a review of all programmes with an energy element. The paper states the overriding objective of the review is to bring together all Community actions for energy into a coherent and comprehensive framework with two objectives:

- to ensure greater transparency of the Community's energy policy

- to examine ways of increasing the effectiveness of the Community's energy policy, in particular by helping to identify areas where Community actions need to be simplified, better co-ordinated or strengthened.

The Commission is expected to come forward with further proposals by the end of 1997.

Gas Liberalisation

10.3   Negotiations continued on a directive establishing the internal market in gas. On 27 May, the Energy Council held a further orientation debate centred on three key issues; a framework for market opening, take or pay contracts, and emergent markets and regions. On the basis of the views expressed, the Presidency concluded that on market opening a qualitative criteria could form the basis of a compromise. This should include power generators and large industrial users as eligible customers; a minimum and thereafter progressive percentage opening of gas markets; a possibility of member states limiting market opening above a certain level. On the possibility of derogating from the directive in the event of problems with future take or pay contracts, the Presidency concluded that there was support for a system characterised by transparency, well formulated criteria and the involvement of national independent gas authorities and the Commission. On emergent markets, the Presidency concluded that there was broad support for the proposal to allow member states only now developing a gas market and those not directly connected to another EU system and having a single external supplier to derogate from parts of the directive. On emergent regions, there was support for further consideration of an approach whereby regions eligible for derogation's would be listed in an annex.

10.4   The Council recognised the Presidency's proposals as an important step in the right direction and as a good basis for progress in further discussions at a possible second Council on 24 June. The Presidency subsequently decided that insufficient progress had been made to justify holding the second Council.

Renewable Energy

10.5   The Energy Council adopted a Resolution welcoming the Commission's 1996 Green Paper "Energy for the Future: Renewable Sources of Energy" and calling on the Commission to develop a detailed strategy for the promotion of renewables in a White Paper, which is expected before the end of this year. The Commission presented its proposal for an ALTENER II programme to the Council and Parliament.

11. Structural and other Funds

Objective 2

11.1   Negotiations between the Government and the Commission on the Government's thirteen Objective 2 Plans for the UK and Gibraltar for the expenditure of 2,500 million ecu (£1, 696 million) resulted in the Commission adopting twelve new Objective 2 programmes for 1997-1999. Objective 2 of the Structural Funds assists designated industrial and urban areas.

Community Initiatives

11.2   The North Sea Area submitted proposals to the Commission on 10 March and the North Western Metropolitan Area presented proposals on 22 May for programmes under the Interreg II-C Community Initiative, which aims to promote transnational co-operation on spatial planning.

Amsterdam European Council

11.3   The Amsterdam European Council of 16 - 17 June noted with satisfaction that over 90 territorial or local employment pacts would be launched in November. These will include up to ten pilot projects in the UK. The pacts are designed to focus Structural Funds more on job creation.

European Spatial Development Perspective

11.4   The first official draft of the European Spatial Development Perspective, assisting the spatial planning of the European territory, was presented to an informal Ministerial meeting in Noordwijk on 8 - 10 June.

Trans-European Networks (Energy)

11.5   On 11 June the Commission announced the co-financing of feasibility studies for 21 trans-European network projects in the energy sector, at a maximum cost of 7.48 million ecu (£5.07 million). Energy networks contribute to the integration of Europe's gas and electricity grids throughout the European Union, to achieve a single internal energy market, and in the implementation of the Energy Charter Treaty. Four of the 21 feasibility studies are UK based projects covering electricity interconnection between; the UK and Netherlands, the UK and Isle of Man, the UK and Norway and Northern Ireland and the Republic of Ireland.

Trans-European Networks (Telecommunications)

11.6   The Conciliation Committee of the European Council and the Parliament reached political agreement on a joint text for a draft decision on a series of guidelines for trans-European telecommunications networks. The decision on trans-European networks (telecommunications) was adopted on 19 June. The programme aims to help Europe's transition to the Information Society by supporting development of new applications, services, and networks.

Trans-European Networks (Interchange of Data between Administrations (IDA))

11.7   At the end of January the Commission completed a 'Call for Ideas' to contribute to discussions on a replacement for the current three-year programme, which ends on 31 December 1997. IDA is responsible for the development and operation of trans-European telematics networks between member state administrations and European Institutions. IDA networks contribute to the functioning of the single market within twelve sectors. The Commission is working towards following up this exercise with a Communication to the Council and the European Parliament by the end of 1997.

Trans-European Networks (Transport)

11.8   The report of the High-Level Group on Public Private Partnership Financing of trans-European network transport projects was presented to the Transport Council on 17-18 June.

12. Subsidiarity and Better Regulation

12.1   As part of an Anglo-Austrian initiative to identify ways of improving European and domestic legislation for small firms, a seminar on "Improving the Business Environment for Entrepreneurs" was held in Vienna on 24 February. Privatisation, regulatory impact assessment and legislative simplification were amongst the issues discussed. It is intended that this bilateral work will help the UK and Austria make regulatory reform a theme for 1998 when the two countries hold consecutive Presidencies of the European Union.

12.2   At the Internal Market Council on 13 March, the Commission reported on progress in developing proposals to implement the recommendations from the first phase of its Simpler Legislation for the Internal Market (SLIM) initiative. Internal Market Ministers endorsed the Commission's work on SLIM and re-affirmed their support for an extension of the initiative to other areas of Single Market legislation. In May, the Commission launched a second round of SLIM reviews to examine the scope for simplifying legislation in the areas of banking, the collection of external trade statistics (Extrastat), fertilizers and VAT. SLIM teams will report to the Internal Market Council in November. The Commission has also proposed in its Single Market Action Plan a permanent rolling programme of SLIM reviews.

12.3   A conference on "The Quality of European and National Legislation and the Internal Market" was held in The Hague on 24-25 April. Working groups, comprising experts from member states, shared best practice on ways of simplifying existing legislation, assessing the impact of new legislation and improving its quality. Ideas emerging from this event will give impetus to work on better regulation at European and national levels.

12.4   The Intergovernmental Conference (IGC) in Amsterdam on 16-17 June adopted a Protocol on the "Application of the Principle of Subsidiarity and Proportionality". Article 9 of the Protocol requires the Commission to:

> "take duly into account the need for any burden, whether financial or administrative, falling upon the Community, national governments, local authorities, economic operators and citizens, to be minimised and proportionate to the objective to be achieved."

The Commission must also demonstrate that Community objectives can be better achieved at Community rather than national level by "qualitative or, wherever possible, quantitative indicators". The Protocol will have legal force once the Amsterdam Treaty is ratified by all member states. The IGC also adopted a "Declaration on the Quality of Legislation" requiring the Council, European Commission and European Parliament to agree guidelines to improve the quality of drafting of Community legislation.

12.5   The Amsterdam European Council also invited the Commission to set up a Task Force to improve the quality of Community legislation and reduce the administrative burden on European businesses, particularly small and medium sized enterprises. The Commission has created the "Business Environment Simplification Task Force" (BEST) to take this work forward.

12.6   The Commission's Legislative and Administrative Simplification Committee continued its work on improving the business environment for small firms. In April, the Commission adopted a recommendation on facilitating business start-ups, calling on member states to reduce the administrative burden imposed on business start-ups and to make the process more business friendly. Specific measures in the recommendation include establishing single contact points for start-up formalities, simplifying forms, and improving authorisation procedures. Member states will report back on progress in implementing this recommendation in twelve months time. Current work is focusing on problems surrounding the transfer of small firms.

13. Common Foreign and Security Policy (CFSP)

13.1   The General Affairs Council and Political Committee met regularly to consider a range of international issues. Developments in Albania, the Great Lakes Region, former Yugoslavia and the Middle East Peace Process continued to dominate the CFSP agenda, but common approaches were also agreed on conflict prevention in Africa and promoting nuclear transparency.

Joint Actions and Common Positions

13.2   The EU agreed a number of Joint Actions and Common Positions, including:

- a Common Position on Albania to support democracy, stability, free and fair elections, economic reform and provide humanitarian assistance;

- a Common Position imposing EU entry restrictions on certain individuals involved in violent acts in Mostar;

- a Joint Action to help the Palestinian Authority counter terrorist activities in the territories under its control; and

- a Joint Action providing some 75,000 ecu (£51,000) towards the costs of the first Nuclear Suppliers Group seminar on nuclear related export controls.

13.3   EU Ambassadors were withdrawn from Tehran in April, after the Mykonos trial implicated Iran in the murder of 4 Iranian dissidents in Germany. In a declaration of the Council of 29 April, the EU's critical dialogue with Iran was suspended and measures were agreed to exclude Iranian intelligence personnel from EU member states.

13.4   The EU extended or modified several existing Joint Actions or Common Positions, including on:

- Nigeria (extension for a further six months of EU measures adopted in 1993);

- Burma (extension for a further six months of EU measures adopted in 1996);

- Bosnia and Herzegovina (continuation of support for the electoral process);

- Dual use goods (updating lists subject to EC export controls).

13.5   The EU also issued 70 declarations and statements on some 50 countries and issues in the framework of CFSP. These included urging a return to constitutional government in Sierra Leone, underlining EU support for continuing democracy in Hong Kong and for free and fair elections to a new Legislative Council, and declarations welcoming elections in El Salvador, Nicaragua and the Gambia. See Appendix C.

14. Justice and Home Affairs

Immigration and Asylum

14.1   The Justice and Home Affairs Council on 26-27 May agreed on the rules and procedures for the Committee set up under the Dublin Convention to decide on the state responsible for examining applications for asylum lodged in one of the EU's member states. The same Council also agreed conclusions about the practical implementation of the Convention which enabled it to enter into force on 1 September 1997.

14.2   The same Council also adopted a Resolution on unaccompanied third-country national minors, a decision on monitoring the implementation of instruments already adopted concerning asylum and a decision on the exchange of information between member states which have programmes of assistance for the voluntary repatriation of third-country nationals. The Council also approved a guide, for use by the countries of Central and Eastern Europe, on effective practices for control of persons at external frontiers.

Organised Crime

14.3   The Justice and Home Affairs Council on 28 April considered and endorsed the 30 specific recommendations contained in the Action Plan of the High Level Group on Organised Crime. The plan puts the emphasis on practical measures, including more effective implementation of existing instruments, improved co-operation with the EU's main partners, in particular with applicant countries, and balancing legislative approximation or harmonisation, where necessary, with practical co-operation between law enforcement agencies.

14.4   The Justice and Home Affairs Council on 26-27 May noted the report from the co-ordinator of the Europol Drugs Unit (EDU), and approved the EDU budget for 1998. The same Council also noted a report on the Europol computer system, and agreed on rules governing the handling of Europol's analysis files, and staff regulations applicable to those employed by Europol.

14.5   Member states on 19 June signed a Protocol to the Europol Convention, which lays down the extent to which Europol staff will benefit from certain privileges and immunities when carrying out their official functions.

Drugs

14.6   The problem of synthetic drugs was given high priority under the Dutch Presidency. The Council on 16-17 June agreed a Joint Action aimed at establishing a mechanism for identifying and controlling new synthetic drugs throughout the EU on the basis of rapid exchange of information on new synthetic drugs emerging in member states and an assessment of their risks. Work also continued on taking forward the drugs strategy agreed at the Madrid European Council.

Police Co-operation

14.7   The Justice and Home Affairs Council on 26-27 May adopted a Joint Action on public order issues aimed at strengthening police co-operation between the member states in policing major events such as sporting events, rock concerts and demonstrations. The Council on 9 June adopted a Resolution on preventing and restraining football hooliganism through the exchange of experience, exclusion from stadia and a comprehensive media policy.

14.8   The Council on 9 June adopted a Resolution on the exchange of DNA analysis results, and encouraged member states to establish national DNA databases with common standards.

Fraud and Corruption

14.9   Member states on 19 June signed a third Protocol to the Convention on the Protection of the Communities' Financial Interests. The Protocol lays down steps to be taken by member states to criminalise a number of offences related to fraud against the Community budget, which were not covered by the parent convention. It includes provisions on money laundering, search and seizure, and liability of legal persons.

14.10 Member states on 26 May signed the Convention on the Fight Against Corruption involving Officials of the European Communities or Officials of the Member States of the European Union.

Judicial Co-operation

14.11 At the Justice and Home Affairs Council on 26 May member states signed a Convention on the Service in Member States of Judicial and Extra Judicial Documents in Civil and Commercial Matters, including a Protocol covering the jurisdiction in these matters of the European Court of Justice.

14.12 The Council on 24 February agreed a joint action concerning measures to combat trafficking in human beings and sexual exploitation of children.

Terrorism

14.13 On 26-27 May the Justice and Home Affairs Council considered a report on terrorist threats to member states.

Customs Co-operation

14.14 The Customs Co-operation Working Group continued with work begun by the Irish Presidency to develop a common external frontier strategy following the recommendations made by the expert group on drugs to the Madrid European Council. Work progressed on a number of issues, including revision of the Naples Convention, joint Customs surveillance exercises and a Third Pillar Customs 2000 joint action. On 9 June the Council adopted a Resolution setting guidelines for joint Customs surveillance operations as well as a joint action on risk analysis.

Racism and Xenophobia

14.15 The Council on 2-3 June agreed that the European Monitoring Centre on Racism and Xenophobia would be established in Vienna.

Co-operation with Third Countries

14.16 Priority was given to relations with future candidates for accession. The structured dialogue concentrated on asylum, and covered in particular the application of the 'safe third country' concept, public attitudes to asylum and the handling of the media. It also covered the possibility of a parallel convention to the Dublin Convention, which would create a procedure for determining the state responsible for examining applications for asylum between EU member states and other contracting parties outside the Union.

14.17 The President of the Justice and Home Affairs Council, Mrs Winnie Sorgdrager, visited the US in the context of the transatlantic dialogue. An EU/US summit took place on 28 May, at which organised crime was one of the major topics. Broad themes for continued co-operation with the US will include anti-terrorism, ongoing implementation of the Caribbean Drugs Initiative, and tackling illicit drug smuggling, especially in relation to the Central and Eastern European countries.

15. Parliamentary Scrutiny of EC Legislation

15.1 549 European Community documents were deposited in Parliament. The diagrams below provide details of how the House of Commons Select Committee on European Legislation (European Legislation Committee) and the House of Lords Select Committee on the European Communities (European Communities Committee) reported on documents considered during the period 1 January-30 June.

House of Commons

Not Legally or Political Important:
128 documents

For debate:
7 documents

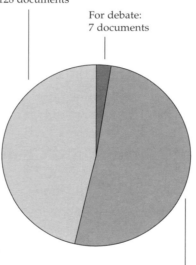

Legal and Political Importance
but not for debate: 141 documents

House of Lords

For further consideration in Sub-Committee:
122 documents

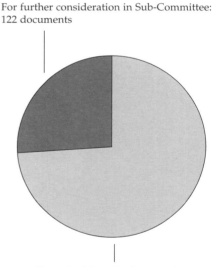

Cleared without further scrutiny:
344 documents

15.2 Seven debates on European Community documents were held in the House of Commons; two in European Standing Committee A, and five in European Standing Committee B. The European Legislation Committee published nine reports on documents which it had considered (see diagram above).

15.3 The European Communities Committee published nine reports, five for information of the House and four for debate. Four reports were debated.

15.4   Further information about scrutiny debates in both Houses, and reports published by the House of Lords European Communities Committee can be found in Appendices E and F.

Select Committee Enquiries

15.5   The House of Commons Select Committee on Procedure (Procedure Committee) published a report in March on the way in which the House deals with European Business (3rd report, 1996-97). The Report from the European Legislation Committee on the Scrutiny of European Business which was published in July 1996, (27th Report, 1995-96) provided the background for the Procedure Committee's deliberations. The Government deferred a response to both reports in the light of the imminent General Election.

15.6   The European Communities Committee conducted an enquiry into the way the Committee was able to scrutinise documents emerging under the Third Pillar of the European Union (Justice and Home Affairs). A report was subsequently published on 12 September (6th Report, 1997-98).

Appendix A: Major Proposals Adopted

Economic and Budgetary

Council Regulation 1103/97 concerning certain provisions relating to the introduction of the euro. Adopted 17 June. (See paragraph 3.9).

Council Regulation 1466/97 on the strengthening of the surveillance of budgetary positions and the surveillance and co-ordination of economic policies. Adopted 7 July. (See paragraph 3.4).

Council Regulation 1467/97 on speeding up and clarifying the implementation of the excessive deficit procedure. Adopted 7 July. (See paragraph 3.20).

Council Directive 97/5/EC on Cross-Border Credit Transfers. Adopted 27 January. (See paragraph 3.21).

European Parliament and Council Directive 97/9/EC on investor-compensation schemes. Adopted 3 March. (See paragraph 3.24).

Agriculture and Food

Council Regulation 154/97 amending Regulation (EEC) 619/71 laying down general rules for granting aid for flax and hemp. Adopted 20 January.

Council Regulation 724/97 determining measures and compensation relating to appreciable revaluations that affect farm incomes. Adopted 22 April.

Council Regulation 820/97 establishing a system for the identification and registration of bovine animals and regarding the labelling of beef products. Adopted 21 April.

Council Regulation 1221/97 laying down general rules for the application of measures to improve the production and marketing of honey. Adopted 23-25 June.

Council Regulation 1255/97 concerning Community criteria for staging points and amending the route plan referred to in the Annex to Directive 91/628/EEC. Adopted 25 June.

Council Directive 97/2 amending Directive 91/629/EEC laying down minimum standards for the protection of calves. Adopted 20 January.

Council Directive 97/3/EC amending Directive 77/93/EEC on protective measures against the introduction into the Community of organisms harmful to plants or plant products and against their spread within the Community. Amendments provide for limited Community contribution to member states' costs in plant pest eradication. Adopted 20 January.

Council Directive 97/12 amending and updating Directive 64/432/EEC on health problems affecting intra-Community trade in bovine animals and swine. Adopted 17 March.

Council Directive 97/41 amending Directives 76/895/EEC, 86/362/EEC, 86/363/EEC and 90/642/EEC concerning pesticides maximum residue levels. Adopted 25 June.

Fisheries

Council Regulation 408/97 on the conclusion of an agreement on co-operation in the sea fisheries sector between the European Community and the Islamic Republic of Mauritania and laying down provisions for its implementation. Adopted 24 February.

Council Regulation 551/97 EC amending Regulation 390/97 fixing for certain fish stocks and groups of fish stocks, the total allowable catches for 1997 and certain conditions under which they may be fished. Adopted 25 March.

Council Regulation 711/97 EC amending, for the second time, Regulation 390/97 fixing for certain fish stocks and groups of fish stocks, the total allowable catches for 1997 and certain conditions under which they may be fished. Adopted 14 April.

Council Regulation 712/97 setting up a specific measure in favour of cephalopod producers permanently based in the Canary Islands. Adopted 22 April.

Council Regulation 779/97 EC introducing arrangements for the management of fishing effort in the Baltic Sea.

Council Regulation 894/97 EC laying down certain technical measures for the conservation of fishery resources. Adopted 29 April.

Council Regulation 909/97 EC on the conclusion of the Protocol establishing, for the period 1 January 1996 to 31 December 1997, the fishing rights and financial compensation provided for in the agreement between the European Economic Community and the Government of the Republic of Guinea on fishing off the Guinean coast. Adopted 14 May.

Council Regulation 910/97 EC on the conclusion of the Protocol defining, for the period from 3 May 1996 to 2 May 1999, the fishing opportunities and the financial compensation provided for by the agreement between the European Economic Community and the Government of the People's Republic of Angola on fishing off the coast of Angola. Adopted 14 May.

Council Regulation 965/97 opening and providing for the management of autonomous Community tariff quotas for certain live fish originating in the Slovak Republic and the Czech Republic.

Council Decision 97/413 concerning the objectives and detailed rules for restructuring the Community fisheries sector for the period from 1 January 1997 to 31 December 2001 with a view to achieving a balance on a sustainable basis between resources and their exploitation.

Council Decision on the conclusion of an agreement in the form of an exchange of letters on the provisional application of the protocol fixing, for the period 1 December 1996 to 30 November 1999, the fishing opportunities and the financial compensation provided for in the Agreement between the European Economic Community and the Government of Mauritius on fishing in Mauritian waters. Adopted 20 May.

Environment

Council Regulation 120/97 amending Regulation (EC) 259/93 on the supervision and control of shipments of waste within, into and out of the European Community. Adopted 20 January.

Council Directive 97/11/EC amending Directive 85/337/EEC on the assessment of the effects of certain public and private projects on the environment. Adopted 3 March.

Council Decision establishing a reciprocal exchange of information and data from networks and individual stations measuring ambient air pollution within the member states. Adopted 27 January.

Consumer

Council Directive 97/7/EC on the protection of consumers in respect of distant contracts (the Distance Selling Directive). The Directive covers transactions between suppliers and consumers for goods and services negotiated and concluded without face-to-face communication (e.g. by mail order, telephone selling, or electronic communication), and gives the consumer rights to prior information and to a cancellation period. Adopted 23 January.

Council Directive 97/37/EC on textile names (the Textile Names Directive). The Directive amends Council Directive 96/74/EC on textile names by adding four new fibre names to the list of permitted generic names for use in fibre content indications relating to textile products. Adopted 19 June.

Transport

Directive 97/24/EC of the European Parliament and of the Council on certain Components and Characteristics of Two or Three-wheeled Vehicles. Adopted 17 June.

Appendix B: Major Treaties and Agreements

Signed by the Member States

Miscellaneous

Protocol, drawn up on the basis of Article K.3 of the Treaty on European Union, on the interpretation, by the Court of Justice of the European Community, of the Convention on the Service in the member states of the European Union of Judicial and Extrajudicial Documents in Civil or Commercial Matters.

Signed in Brussels, 26 May 1997

Convention, drawn up on the basis of Article K.3 of the Treaty on European Union, on the Service in the member states of the European Union of Judicial and Extrajudicial Documents in Civil or Commercial Matters.

Signed in Brussels, 26 May 1997

Second Protocol drawn up on the basis of Article K.3 of the Treaty of European Union, to the Convention on the Protection of the European Community's Financial Interests.

Signed in Brussels, 19 June 1997

Signed by the Community and Member States

Moldova

Protocol to the Partnership and Co-operation Agreement, establishing a partnership between the European Community and its member states, on the one part, and the Republic of Moldova, on the other part.

Signed in Brussels, 15 May 1997

Romania

Amending Protocol No.4 to the Europe Agreement establishing an association between the European Community and its member states, on the one part, and Romania on the other part.

Signed in Brussels, 31 January 1997

Russian Federation

Protocol to the Agreement on Partnership and Co-operation, establishing a partnership between the European Community and its member states, on the one part, and the Russian Federation on the other part.

Signed in Brussels, 21 May 1997

Ukraine

Protocol to the Partnership and Co-operation Agreement, between the European Community and its member states, on the one part, and Ukraine on the other part.

Signed in Brussels, 10 April 1997

"Community Alone" Treaties

Angola

Agreement in the form of an Exchange of Letters concerning the provisional application of the Protocol defining for the period from 3 May 1996 to 2 May 1999 the fishing opportunities and the financial compensation provided for by the Agreement between the European Economic Community and the Government of the People's Republic of Angola on fishing off the coast of Angola.

Signed in Brussels, 24 September 1996

Cyprus

Agreement in the form of an Exchange of Letters between the European Community and Cyprus on the adjustment of the regime for imports into the European Community of oranges originating in Cyprus.

Signed in Brussels, 1 December 1996

European Free Trade Area (EFTA)

Exchange of Letters recording the common understanding on the principles of international co-operation on research and development activities in the domain of intelligent manufacturing systems between the European Community and the United States of America, Japan, Australia, Canada and the EFTA countries of Norway and Switzerland.

Signed in Brussels, 19 March 1997

Korea

Agreement between the European Community and the Republic of Korea on co-operation and mutual administrative assistance in customs matters.

Signed in Brussels, 10 April 1997

Mauritania

Agreement in the form of Exchange of Letters concerning the provisional application of the Agreement on co-operation in the sea fisheries sector between the European Community and the Islamic Republic of Mauritania.

Signed in Brussels, 20 October 1996

Mauritius

Protocol fixing, for the period 1 December 1996 to 30 November 1999, the fishing opportunities and the financial consideration provided for in the Agreement between the European Economic Community and the Government of Mauritius on fishing in Mauritian waters.

Signed in Brussels, 1 December 1996

Agreement in the form of an Exchange of Letters on the provisional application of the Protocol fixing, for the period 1 December 1996 to 30 November 1999, the fishing opportunities and the financial consideration provided for in the Agreement between the European Economic Community and the Government of Mauritius on fishing in Mauritian waters.

Signed in Brussels, 20 May 1997

Norway

Agreement on customs co-operation in the form of an Exchange of Letters between the European Community and the Kingdom of Norway (with Exchange of Notes).

Signed in Brussels, 10 April 1997

Palestine Authority

Euro-Mediterranean Interim Agreement on Trade and Co-operation between the European Community, on the one part, and the Palestine Liberation Organisation (PLO) for the benefit of the Palestine Authority of the West Bank and the Gaza Strip, on the other part.

Signed in Brussels, 24 February 1997

Agreement in the form of an Exchange of Letters between the Community and the Palestine Authority relating to Article 1 of Protocol 1 and concerning imports into the Community of fresh cut flowers and flower buds falling within subhead 060310 of the Common Customs Tariff.

Signed in Brussels, 24 February 1997

Switzerland

Agreement in the form of an Exchange of Letters between the European Community and the Swiss Confederation adding to the Agreement between the European Economic Community and the Swiss Confederation a protocol on mutual administrative assistance in customs matters.

Signed in Luxembourg, 2 June 1997

United States of America

Agreement between the European Community and the United States of America on Co-operation regarding the Control of Precursors and Chemical Substances frequently used in the Illicit Manufacture of Narcotic Drugs or Psychotropic Substances.

Signed in Brussels, 21 May 1997

Appendix C: European Union Declarations and Statements

9 January		Former Yugoslavia
10 January		Central African Republic
21 January		Germany/Czech Republic
23 January	*	Nicaragua
24 January		Bulgaria
27 January		The Gambia
31 January	*	Chechnya
3 February		Angola
4 February	*	Central African Republic
5 February	*	Niger
11 February		Croatia
13 February	*	Iran
15 February		Bosnia
17 February		Ecuador
17 February		Zaire
18 February		Republic of Korea
24 February		China
27 February		Israel
3 March		Burma
3 March		Swaziland
7 March	*	Albania
7 March		Zaire
10 March		Former Yugoslav Republic of Macedonia
11 March		El Salvador
13 March	*	Tajikistan
13 March		Albania
17 March		Albania
17 March		Zaire
25 March		Mostar
25 March	*	Liberia
9 April		Cambodia
10 April		Iran
10 April		Zaire
11 April		Angola
14 April		Peru/Ecuador
17 April	*	Sri Lanka
29 April		Croatia
29 April		Former Yugoslavia
29 April		Belarus
29 April	*	Iran
30 April	*	El Salvador
7 May		Burundi
7 May		Cameroon
13 May	*	Moldova-Transdniestria
14 May		Afghanistan
16 May	*	Russia-Chechnya
16 May		Turkey
16 May		Albania
20 May		Burundi

21 May		Convention on Chemical Weapons
22 May		Democratic Republic of Congo
27 May		Korean Peninsula
28 May	*	Sierra Leone
29 May	*	Convention on Chemical Weapons
30 May		Yemen
30 May		Slovakia
30 May		Myanmar/Burma
2 June		Romania/Ukraine
2 June		ASEAN
5 June	*	Russia/Ukraine
10 June		Algeria
13 June	*	Columbia
18 June	*	Kosovo
20 June	*	Colombia
20 June		Mali
20 June		Sierra Leone
20 June		Congo (Brazzaville)
20 June	*	Albania
30 June		Hong Kong
30 June		India/Pakistan

* Declarations with which the Associate Countries, Cyprus and the EFTA/EEA were associated.

Appendix D, Part 1: List of European Court of Justice cases involving the United Kingdom

This list includes all cases awaiting judgment and those in which judgment was received during the period. An asterisk denotes those cases in which the United Kingdom applied to intervene or submitted Observations/Pleadings during the period.

(i) Actions initiated by the United Kingdom under Article 173 of the EC Treaty.

1. **C-150/94 : United Kingdom -v- Council**
Application seeking the annulment of Council Regulation 519/94 in so far as it imposes quantitative quotas on three categories of toys originating in China.

2. **C-274/94 : United Kingdom -v- Commission**
Seeking the annulment of Commission Decision C23/94 of 27 July 1994 on the increased capitalization of Air France. Stayed pending decision of CFI in T371/94 (British Airways & Others -v- Commission).

3. **C180/96 and C180/96R: United Kingdom -v- Commission**
Seeking the annulment of Commission Decision 96/239/EC on the export of British beef and beef products and relative application for interim measures.

4. **C-106/96, C-239/96, C-240/96, C-305/96 : United Kingdom -v- Commission**
By these actions the UK is seeking the annulment of certain Commission decisions concerning expenditure on the ground that they lack legal base.

(ii) Direct actions against the United Kingdom under Article 169 of the EC Treaty.

1. **C-300/95 : Commission -v- United Kingdom**
Directive 85/374 liability for defective products. The Commission alleges that the UK has failed to implement correctly Article 7(e). Judgment 29 May. See Part 2 of this Appendix.

2. **C-340/96 : Commission -v- United Kingdom**
Directive 80/778/EEC on the quality of water intended for human consumption. The Commission alleges that the UK has failed to implement this directive correctly in relation to arrangements for enforcing compliance by water companies and maximum admissible concentrations.

(iii) Cases referred to the European Court under Article 177 of the EC Treaty from United Kingdom courts or tribunals.

1. **C-27/95 : Woodspring District Council -v- Bakers of Nailsea**
Veterinary inspection fees: Directive 91/497. Judgment 15 April. See Part 2 of this Appendix.

2. **C-40/95 : Conoco -v- Commissioners of Customs & Excise**
Sixth VAT Directive - "Money-off" coupons. Withdrawn.

3.   C-65/95 : Secretary of State for the Home Department, ex parte Shingara
Council Directive 64/221/EEC - exclusion of EC nationals on national security grounds.
Joined with C111/95. Judgment 17 June. See Part 2 of this Appendix.

4.   C-66/95 : R -v- Secretary of State for Social Security ex parte Eunice Sutton
Directive 79/7 - equal treatment for men and women in matters of social security - right to
receive interest on arrears of benefits. Judgment 22 April. See Part 2 of this Appendix.

5.   C-110/95 : Yamanouchi Pharmaceutical Co. Ltd -v- Comptroller-General of Patents,
Designs & Trade Marks
Entitlement to a supplementary protection certificate under Regulation 1768/92. Judgment 12
June.

6.   C-111/95 : R -v- Secretary of State for the Home Department, ex parte Radiom
Council Directive 64/221/EEC - exclusion of EC nationals on national security grounds.
Joined with C65/95. Judgment 17 June. See Part 2 of this Appendix.

7.   C-124/95 : R -v- HM Treasury ex parte Centro-Comm & Bank of England
Article 113 EC and Council Regulation 1432/92 prohibiting trade between the Community and
Serbia and Montenegro. Judgment 14 January. See Part 2 of this Appendix.

8.   C-127/95 : Norbrook Laboratories Ltd -v- MAFF
Conditions for the licensing of veterinary medicinal products; Directives 81/851 and 81/852.
Joined with C-29/96.

9.   C-165/95 : R -v- MAFF ex parte Lay and Gage & Gage
Calculation of the special reference quantity of milk pursuant to Reg 2055/93 (SLOM III).

10.   C-260/95 : Commissioners of Customs & Excise -v- DFDS A/S
Sixth VAT Directive - the liability to VAT of a Danish travel agent in respect of activities of its
UK agent. Judgment 20 February.

11.   C-296/95 : R -v- HM C & E, ex parte EMU TABAC
Directive 92/12/EEC (excise duty on tobacco products) - whether imports effected by an
agent are "personal" imports qualifying for exemption from duty.

12.   C-330/95 : R -v- Commissioners of HM Customs & Excise ex parte Goldsmiths
The Sixth VAT Directive: the scope of the derogation in Article 11C1, and whether it permits
member states which have enacted provisions for the refund of tax in the case of bad debts
to exclude relief where the consideration lost is not monetary.

13.   C-339/95 : Compagnia Di Navigazione Marittima
Arbitral awards - whether these are "agreements" for the purpose of Article 85 EC. If so,
whether enforcement of such an award might constitute a breach of that Article.

14.   C-345/95 : R -v- MAFF ex parte NFU
Concerning the validity of Regulation 3887/92 establishing an integrated administration and
control scheme for certain Community aid schemes (ie arable area payments scheme and the
Beef Special Premium Scheme and the Suckler Cow Premium Scheme).

15.   C-1/96 : R -v- MAFF ex parte RSPCA
Export of live veal calves.

16.   C-4/96 : NIFPO -v- DANI
Whether the Hague Preference is ultra vires the Common Fisheries Policy.

17.   C-20/96 : Kelvin Snares -v- Adjudication Officer

Concerning the interpretation of Regulation 1408/71 (as amended by Regulation 1247/92) - whether certain classes of invalidity benefit are exportable.

18.   C-29/96 : Norbrook -v- MAFF

Whether the UK has properly implemented Directives 81/851 and 81/852 - the licensing of veterinary medicinal products. Joined with C-127/95.

19.   C-82/96 : R -v- Secretary of State for Trade and Industry ex parte the Consumers Association and Which

The High Court has referred questions concerning the interpretation of Council Directive 93/13 on unfair terms in consumer contracts in the light of the Unfair Terms in Consumer Contracts Regulations 1994. In particular they challenge the implementation of Article 7(2) of the Directive which identifies the category of persons or organisations which can challenge unfair terms in consumer contracts.

20.   C-157/96 : The Queen -v- MAFF & HM Customs & Excise -v- ex parte NFU and Others

This reference arises from the judicial review brought by the NFU in respect of UK measures implementing Commission Decision 96/239 which imposed the ban on export of British beef and beef products. The Divisional Court asks whether that Decision is valid. Heard with C-180/96: UK -v- Commission.

21.   C-171/96 : Roque -v- Lieutenant Governor of Jersey

Reference from the Royal Court of Jersey concerning the deportation of a Portuguese national.

22.   C-172/96 : Commissioners of Customs & Excise -v- First National Bank of Chicago

The High Court has referred questions asking the ECJ to rule on whether foreign exchange transactions constitute the supply of goods and services and, if so, what is the nature of the consideration provided in that supply.

23.   C-246/96 : Magorrian -v- Eastern Health and Social Services Board

The Industrial Tribunal in Northern Ireland has referred questions regarding the interpretation of Community Equal Pay legislation and Community rules on national limitations on the back dating of entitlements in the event of a successful claim.

24.   C-249/96 : Grant -v- South West Trains

Article 119 EC and Directive 75/117 concerning concessionary travel not being available for a partner of the same sex as the applicant.

25.   C-264/96 : ICI -v- Colmer

Article 52 EC concerning a disputed claim for consortium relief under the Income and Corporation Taxes Act 1970.

26.   C-297/96 : Vera Partridge -v- Adjudication Officer

This case is very similar to case C-20/96: Kelvin Snares noted above. Both references concern the interpretation of Regulation 1408/71 and the exportability of certain types of disability benefits.

27.   C-308/96 : The Commissioners & Customs & Excise -v- Madgett & Baldwin

Concerns the interpretation of the Sixth VAT Directive, in particular, the criteria to be applied in determining whether a person making supplies of travel and accommodation is to be regarded as a tour operator or travel agent.

28. *C-326/96 : Mrs B S Levez -v- T H Jennings (Harlow Pools) Ltd
Whether the 2 years' arrears limit in the Equal Pay Act is compatible with Community law.

29. *C-349/96 : Card Protection Plan -v- Commissioners for Customs & Excise
Article 13(B)(a) of the Sixth VAT Directive. Whether the provision of a service consisting of insuring against loss of credit cards and various ancillary services is subject to VAT.

30. *C-368/96 : Medicines Control Agency ex parte Generics (UK) Ltd
Council Directive 65/65 on the granting of marketing authorisations for medicinal products. An abbreviated procedure applies where a licence is sought in relation to a product which is "essentially similar" to a product for which authorisation has already been granted. The High Court seeks guidance as to the interpretation of this phrase.

31. *C-349/96 : Mary Brown -v- Rentokil (UK) Ltd
Concerns the Equal Treatment Directive and the lawfulness of dismissing a women on the grounds of absence due to ill health arising from pregnancy.

32. *C-411/96 : M Boyle & Others -v- Equal Opportunities Commission
Concerns the compatibility with Article 119, the Equal Pay and Treatment Directives and the Pregnant Workers Directive with various conditions of employment concerning maternity, in particular conditions concerning accrual of annual leave, pensionable service and the inter-relationship between paid sick and paid maternity leave.

33. *C-416/96 : Nour Eddine El Yassini -v- Secretary of State for the Home Department
EC/Morocco Co-operation Agreement. The case turns upon whether the prohibition against discrimination regarding "working conditions" in Article 40 of the Agreement extends to security of employment and, consequently, confers a right of residence.

34. * C-3/97: R -v- HM Customs & Excise ex parte John Charles Goodwin and Edwin Thomas Unstead
Concerns whether the supply of counterfeit perfume products falls within the scope of the Sixth VAT Directive.

35. * C-47/97 : The Vehicle Inspectorate -v- E Clarke & Sons (Coaches) Ltd and D J Ferne
Council Regulation 684/92 on driving hours, etc. Whether the Regulation applies to groups of passengers carried on a single journey between an airport and a hotel via, on occasions, a tourist attraction.

36. *C-48/97 : Kuwait Petroleum
The Sixth VAT Directive. Whether redemption goods provided in exchange for vouchers obtained on the purchase of premium goods in a business promotion scheme are to be classified as free gifts incurring VAT for the promoter.

37. *C-85/97 : SPRL Société Financière D'Investissements, S.F.I. -v- État Belge
Sixth VAT Directive. The principal issue in this case concerns the treatment of benefits in kind granted to employees.

38. *C-90/97 : Robin Swaddling -v- Adjudication Officer
Concerns the compatibility with Article 48 of the EC Treaty of the UK condition of habitual residence in relation to entitlement to income support.

39. *C-94/97 : T P Madgett and R M Baldwin trading as the Howden Court Hotel -v- Commissioners of Customs & Excise (No. 2)
This is a follow up to case C-308/96 above and concerns the method by which a tour operator's 'margin' is to be calculated when there is a mixed supply of 'in-house' and 'bought-in' services.

40.   *C-120/97 : Upjohn Ltd -v- The Licensing Authority

Directive 65/65 on the granting of marketing authorisations for medicinal products. In this case the Applicant's licence for a particular product was revoked by the Licensing authority on the grounds of safety. The Applicant contents that by virtue of the Directive and Community law generally it is entitled to a full appeal on the facts to a court of law rather than the limited right of review provided for in the Medicines Act.

(iv) Cases referred to the European Court under Article 177 of the EC Treaty from other Member States' courts or tribunals in which Observations have been submitted by the United Kingdom.

1.   C-90/94 : Haahr Petroleum Ltd -v- Aabenraa Havn and others

Articles 9-13,84(2) and 95 of the EEC Treaty: Import surcharge on goods from another member State-limitation period - Emmott.

2.   C-105/94 : Ditta Angelo Celestini -v- Saar Sekskellerei Faber GmbH & Co. KG

Concerns the compatibility with Articles 30 and 36 of the EC Treaty of subjecting wines from other member states to analysis of composition to check that they have not been watered down. Judgment 5 June.

3.   C-313/94 : Ayse Suzen -v- Firma Zehmcker Gebandereiniging

Directive 77/187 : safeguarding of employee's rights with respect of a transfer of a business. Judgment 11 March. See Part 2 of this Appendix.

4.   C-340/94 : De Jaeck -v- Staatssecretaris Van Financien

Articles 13 and 14 of Regulation 1408/71 and the liability for social security contributions of persons employed in one member state and self-employed in another. Judgment 30 January.

5.   C-1/95 : Hellen Gerster -v- Freistaat Bayern

Article 119 and Equal Pay and Equal Treatment Directives : indirect discrimination : rules for calculating seniority of part-time workers.

6.   C-2/95 : Sparekassernes Datacenter -v- Ministry for Fiscal Affairs

Sixth VAT Directive : scope of exclusion of banking services : ancillary activities such as data processing. Judgment 5 June. See Part 2 of this Appendix.

7.   C-94/95 & C-95/95 : Bonifaci & Ors -v- INPS

Council Directive 80/987/EC (insolvency of employers) - whether properly implemented by Italy - minimum guarantees established by the Directive.

8.   C-120/95 : Decker -v- Caisse de Maladie des Employés Privés

Article 30 of the EC Treaty - rules relating to the cost of reimbursement of medical accessories.

9.   C-132/95 : Bent Jensen -v- Landbrugsministeriet

Set off of an amount due to the beneficiary of aid under a Community measure against outstanding debts to a member state.

10.   C-136/95 : CNAVTS -v- Thibault

Directive 76/207 (equal treatment): maternity leave and performance assessment.

11.　　C-147/95 : D.E.I -v- Evrenopoulos

Article 119 EC and Directive 79/7 in relation to survivor's benefits under a pension scheme established by law for employees of the Public Electricity Company, a State body. Judgment 17 April.

12.　　C-171/95 : Tetik -v- Land Berlin

EEC/Turkey Association Agreement. Judgment 23 January.

13.　　C-177/95 : Ebony Maritime SA -v- Prefetto della Provincia di Brindisi, Ministero dell 'Interno

Decision 93/235 concerning trade between the EC and Serbia and Montenegro. Judgment 27 February. See Part 2 of this Appendix.

14.　　C-188/95 : Fantask -v- Industriministeriet

Council Directive 69/335 concerning indirect taxes on the raising of capital.

15.　　C-222/95 : Societe Parodi -v- Banque Albert de Bary et Cie

Council Directive 89/646/EEC (Second Banking Co-ordination Directive) - whether contrary to Articles 59 and 61 of the EC Treaty to require a bank established in another Member State to be licensed in respect of cross-border banking services.

16.　　C-224/95 : Criminal Proceedings -v- Savini

Interpretation of the term "waste" in Directives 156/91 and 689/91 & Regulation 259/93. Judgment 25 June. See Part 2 of this Appendix.

17.　　C-229/95 : Simone Moll -v- Berhane Mesghena

Whether a cleaning contract relating to specific premises constitutes a part of a business within Directive 77/187 (Acquired Rights Directive).

18.　　C-250/95 : Futura Participations & Singer -v- Administration des Contributions

Article 52 of the EC Treaty - direct taxation - treatment of non-resident companies - whether provisions discriminatory. Judgment 15 May.

19.　　C-251/95 : Sabel BV -v- Puma AG

Council Directive 89/104/EEC (Trade Marks) - "likelihood of confusion" - whether mere association sufficient to constitute an infringement of a registered trademark.

20.　　C-258/95 : Julius Fillibeck Sohne GmbH & Co. Ltd -v- Finanzamt Neustadt

Sixth VAT Directive - transport services provided free of charge by an employer to his employees.

21.　　C-261/95 : Palmisani -v- INPS

Council Directive 80/987/EC (insolvency of employers) - whether properly implemented by Italy - claims for Francovich damages - appropriate national time limits.

22.　　C-283/95 : Fischer -v- Finanzamt Danaveschingen

Sixth VAT Directive - unauthorised games of chance.

23.　　C-285/95 : Suat Kol -v- Land Berlin

EEC/Turkey Association Agreement. Judgment 5 June.

24.　　C-299/95 : Kremzow -v- Republic of Austria

Whether the European Convention for the Protection of Human Rights forms part of Community law with the result that the ECJ has jurisdiction to give a preliminary ruling under Article 177 on the interpretation of the Convention. Judgment 29 May.

25.   C-316/95 : Generics BV -v- Smith Kline French Laboratories
Whether Article 30 precludes the grant by national courts of certain forms of injunctive relief in proceedings for enforcement of intellectual property rights.

26.   C-323/95 : Hayes -v- Kronenberger
Whether a German procedural rule providing that foreign plaintiffs are required to give security for costs unless there is a reciprocal agreement between Germany and the plaintiff's state of nationality, is contrary to Article 6 EC Treaty. Judgment 20 March.

27.   C-337/95 : Parfums Christian Dior
Directive 89/104/EEC on trade marks. Can the proprietor of a trade mark prohibit the use of his mark by third parties in relation to the advertisement of goods placed on the market with his consent?

28.   C-343/95 : Diego Cali & Figli Srl -v- Servizi Ecologi Porti di Genova SpA (SEPG)
Concerning the compatibility with Article 86 of charges made by a port authority in respect of anti-pollution services. Judgment 18 March. See Part 2 of this Appendix.

29.   C-349/95 : F Loendersloot -v- Ballantine & Son
Articles 30 & 36 and the exercise of intellectual property rights. Can the proprietor of a trade mark prohibit the re-affixing of his mark where the new labels omit information or introduce a new description of the product?

30.   C-364 & C-365/95 : T Port -v- Hauptzollamt Hamburg-Jonas
Bananas - Regulation 404/93 - whether the provisions of GATT take precedence over Community law in the Federal Republic of Germany.

31.   C-373/95 : Maso & Others -v- INPS
Concerning the implementation by Italy of the Insolvency Directive - whether the Italian legislation falls within the scope of the derogations permitted by the Directive.

32.   C-400/95 : Elisabeth Larsson
Whether Directive 76/207 (Equal Treatment) covers dismissal after maternity leave where the illness was partly attributable to pregnancy related illness before maternity leave. Judgment 29 May. See Part 2 of this Appendix.

33.   C-409/95 : Marschall -v- Land Nordrhein Westfalen
Concerning the interpretation of the Equal Treatment Directive - the lawfulness of rules providing for positive discrimination in favour of women for posts in which women are under represented.

34.   C-14/96 : Criminal Proceedings against Denuit
The jurisdiction of member states under the "Television without Frontiers" Directive 89/552. Judgment 29 May. See Part 2 of this Appendix.

35.   C-17/96 : Badische Erfrischungsgetraenke
Whether Germany has properly implemented Directive 80/777 on the marketing of natural mineral water.

36.   C-19/96 : Casano -v- Inami
Regulation 1408/71.

37.   C-50/96 : Schroder -v- Deutsche Bundesport Telekom
Article 119 EC : exclusion of certain part-time employees from an occupational pension scheme.

38.   C-53/96 : Hermes -v- FHT

The interpretation of Article 50 TRIPS. UK's view is that the ECJ has no jurisdiction to determine the questions referred.

39.   C-66/96 : Pedersen -v- FBD

Pay during absence from work on grounds of illness, outside the maternity leave period.

40.   C-118/96 : Safir

Tax on insurance premiums.

41.   C-121/96 : Bulut

Acquired Rights Directive.

42.   C-127/96 : Hernandez Vidal

Acquired Rights Directive.

43.   C-129/96 : ASBL -v- Region Wallonie

Directive 75/442 : Waste.

44.   C-141/96 : Finanzamt Osnabruck -v- Langhorst

In this German reference, the Court is asked to interpret Article 22(3)(c) of the 6th VAT Directive, and, in particular, whether a credit note can be regarded as an invoice under Article 21(1)(c).

45.   C-158/96 : Kohll -v- UDC

The Luxembourgeous plaintiff in the main proceedings challenges the refusal of his medical insurance company in Luxembourg to reimburse medical costs incurred in Germany. The Insurance company relies on the compatibility of its internal rules with Regulation 1408/71, but the plaintiff alleges that the decision was in breach of Article 59.

46.   C-163/96 : Criminal Proceedings against Silvano Raso

This case concerns the interpretation of Articles 59, 86 and 90(1) of the EC Treaty in the context of Italian legislation on terminal operations in maritime ports. The UK submits that the grant of exclusive rights to an undertaking is not precluded unless the undertaking commits an abuse of a dominant position and the abuse is the inevitable result of that grant.

47.   C-173/96 : Sanchez Hidalgo

Acquired Rights Directive.

48.   C-200/96 : Metronome Musik GmbH and Music Point Hokamp GmbH

The referring Court in this case asks whether the exclusive rental right provided for in Article 1(1) of Council Directive 92/100/EEC is compatible with Community fundamental rights.

49.   C-228/96 : Fallimento Aprile SrL in Liquidazione and Amministrazione delle Finanze

Concerns a claim for repayment of customs duties levied in contravention of Community law; the referring court asks whether a domestic law time limit of three years from the date of payment of the disputed charge is compatible with Community law, having regard to the fact the Civil Code provides for a longer limitation for similar classes of claims.

50.   C-231/96 : Societa Edis and Ministero delle Finanze

This case raises issues similar to those in case C-228/96: Fallimento Aprile. In addition the national court, referring to case C-208/90: Emmott, asks whether national time limits begin to run before the national provision which is inconsistent with Community law is repealed.

51.   Joined cases C-253/96 to C-258/96 : Helmut Kampelmann & Others and Landschaftsverband Westfalen-Lippe
Concerns the interpretation of Council Directive 91/533 on an employer's obligation to inform employees of the conditions applicable to the contract or employment relationship.

52.   C-260/96 : Ministero delle Finanze and SPAC S.P.A.
This case is essentially the same as Case C-228/96: Fallimento Aprile and Case C-231/96: Societa Edis.

53.   C-262/96 : Serul
Decision 80/EEC/Turkey Association Council.

54.   C-279/96 : Ansaldo Energia
See cases C228/96 and C231/96.

55.   C-300/96 : Erika Reimer
Concerns the IACS system and raises issues similar to those in Case C-354/95: R -v- MAFF ex parte NFU.

56.   *C-336/96 : M Et Mme Gilly -v- Directeur des Services Fiscaux du Bas-Rhin
In this case the applicant taxpayers contend that certain provisions of the double taxation agreement between France and Germany are contrary to Community law in that, as a frontier worker, Mme Gilly is liable to pay income tax on her salary in both countries.

57.   *C-343/96 : Dilexport S.r.l. -v- Amministrazione delle Finanze dello Stato
This case raises issues similar to those in Case C-125/94: Aprile and concerns the application of national time limits to claims for reimbursement of sums levied in breach of Community law.

58.   *C-348/96 : Criminal Proceedings against Donatella Calfa
Concerns the compatibility with Community law of an order made by a criminal Court excluding a Community national from Greece .

59.   *C-355/96 : Silhouette International Schmied Gesellschaft GmbH -v- Hartlauer Handelsgesellschaft GmbH
Concerns the interpretation of the Trade Marks Directive (89/104) and the principle of international exhaustion of trade mark rights.

60.   *C-370/96 : Covita A.V.E. -v- Elliniko Dimisio
Concerns the procedures for post clearance of import duties. The issue is whether an error of law on the part of the Customs authorities precludes such recovery.

61.   *C-387/96 : Anders Sjöberg -v- Åklagaren
Council Regulation 3820/85 on driver's hours, etc. Whether the provisions of the Regulation apply to a private company which has contracted to provide public services.

62.   *C-399/96 : Europieces SA in liquidation -v- Winifred Sanders and Others
Concerns the application of the Acquired Rights Directive to transfers made by an undertaking in voluntary liquidation.

63.   *C-400/96 : Criminal Proceedings against Jean Harpegnies
Concerns the compatibility with Article 30 of Belgian legislation which requires approval by the Belgian authorities of plant protection products marketed in another member state.

64.   *C-414/96 : Mechthild Kehrl -v- Allgemeine Ortkrankenkasse Hamburg
Directive 79/7 on equal treatment between men and women in the field of social security.
This case is concerned with the German threshold (18 hours per week) for cover under the
statutory unemployment insurance scheme. The applicant holds two part time jobs but is not
permitted to aggregate her hours of work. She contends that this rule is indirectly
discriminatory.

65.   *C-10/97 : Ministero delle Finanze -v- IN.CO.GE.'90 SrL
Reference from the Italian courts concerning the application of national time limits to claims
for reimbursement of sums levied in contravention of Community law.

66.   *C-33/97 : Colim NV -v- Bigg's Continent Noord NV
Concerns the rules on the labelling of foodstuffs and whether domestic legislation on this
subject might constitute 'technical regulations' within the meaning of Directive 83/189.

67.   *C-34/97 : RWE Engergie AG and Stadt Nordhorn -v- Bundeskartellamt
Concerns the application by the domestic competition authorities of EC competition rules to
the electricity sector. The issues arising include whether national authorities are required to
refrain from applying Article 85 when a common position has been reached concerning rules
for the internal market in electricity and whether such authorities can apply Article 85 pending
a decision by the Commission on negative clearance.

68.   *C-39/97 : Canon Kabushiki Kaisha -v- Pathe Communications Corporation
Raises questions about the interpretation of the Trade Marks Directive, in particular the extent
to which the reputation of an earlier mark is relevant in assessing whether there is a risk of
confusion owing to the degree of similarity between that mark and one for which registration
is sought.

69.   *C-61/97 : Forenigen Af Dansk Videodistributører acting on behalf of Egmont Film
A/S and Others -v- Laserdisken v/Hans Kristian Pedersen
Directive 92/100 on rental rights and copyright. Concerns the distinction between the right of
a copyright holder to distribute copies of a laser disc and the right to authorise the rental of
the disc. In this case the copyright holder distributed copies of a laser disc in the UK and
also authorised their rental. The disc was also distributed in Denmark but the copyright
holder reserved to himself exclusive rental rights in that country. The defendant imported the
disc from the UK and sought to rent it out commercially. The issue is whether the
enforcement by the copyright holder of his exclusive rental right is contrary to Article 30 of the
Treaty.

70.   *C-63/97 : Bayerische Motorwerke AG and Another -v- Ronald Karel Deenik
Concerns the Trade Marks Directive (89/104).   At issue is the legitimacy of the use by a firm
which specialises in the sale of second hand BMWs and the repair of BMWs of the BMW
trade mark in advertising its services.

71.   *C-77/97 : Österreichische Unilever GmbH -v- Smithkline Beecham Markenartikel
GmbH
Concerns the Cosmetic Directive 76/768 - the national court asks whether Member States are
free to impose requirements which are more stringent than those set out in the Directive in
relation to statements in advertising toothpaste which give a misleading view as to the
product's efficacy in combatting tooth decay.

72.   *C-77/97 : Happy Sports Michl OHG -v- Finanzamt Landshut
Sixth VAT Directive. The case concerns the scope of exemptions relating to the hiring of
sports facilities.

(v) Actions in which the United Kingdom intervened in The Court of Justice under Article 37 of the Protocol on the Statute of the Court of Justice.

1.   C-156/94 : Commission -v- Ireland
Articles 30, 34 & 37: State monopoly in respect of the import and export of electricity.

2.   C-157/94 : Commission -v- Netherlands
Articles 30, 34 & 37: State monopoly in respect of the import of electricity.

3.   C-158/94 : Commission -v- Italy
Articles 30, 34 & 37: State monopoly in respect of the import and export of electricity.

4.   C-159/94 : Commission -v- France
Articles 30, 34 & 37: State monopolies in respect of the import and export of gas and electricity.

5.   C-160/94 : Commission -v- Spain
Articles 30, 34 & 37: State monopoly in respect of the import and export of electricity.

6.   C-9/95 : Belgium -v- Commission
An application to annul Regulation 2791/94 in so far as it grants an exceptional allocation of quotas to certain banana producers who suffered loss as a result of tropical storm Debbie. Judgment 4 February. See Part 2 of this Appendix.

7.   C-23/95 : Germany -v- Commission.
Same as C-9/95. Judgment 4 February. See Part 2 of this Appendix.

8.   C-156/95 : Belgium -v- Commission
Same as C-9/95, although in relation to a different production period. Judgment 4 February. See Part 2 of this Appendix.

9.   C-158/95 : Germany -v- Commission
Action under Article 173 for annulment of a Commission Decision relating to state aid to the German steel industry.

10.   C-265/95 : Commission -v- France
Article 169 proceedings concerning the obstruction by criminal acts of the free movement of goods.

11.   C-291/95 : Belgium -v- Commission
Article 173 action concerning State aids in the form of landing fees for Sabena at Brussels national airport.

12.   C-388/95 : Belgium -v- Spain
Belgium challenges Spain's alleged failure to implement the judgment in Case C-47/90: Delhaize, in breach of Article 34 EC Treaty. The Spanish laws in issue in Delhaize which regulate the production of wine were found to constitute a restriction on exports, have not only been maintained in force, but similar laws have been introduced in other regions of Spain. The UK has intervened in support of Belgium.

13.   C-396/95 : Germany -v- Commission
Same issues as C-23/95.

14.   C-399/95 : Germany -v- Commission

Action under Article 173 for the annulment of a Commission Decision relating to state aid to the German steel industry.

15.   C-404/95 : Germany -v- Commission

Action under Article 173 for annulment of a Commission Decision relating to state aid to the German steel industry.

16.   C-407/95 : Belgium -v- Commission

An application to annul Regulation 2358/95 in so far as it grants an exceptional allocation of quotas to certain banana products as a result of tropical storms Iris, Luis and Marilyn.

17.   C-43/96 : Commission -v- France

The Commission challenges France's implementation of the 6th VAT Directive, and the case concerns, in particular, the interpretation of Article 17(6). That provision requires the Council to decide, within 4 years of the date of entry into force of the Directive, what expenditure shall not be eligible for a deduction of VAT. The provision allows member states to maintain in force national regulations concerning the eligibility of expenditure for deduction of VAT in the meantime. The Commission argues that the exception to the principle of entitlement to deduct input tax cannot be interpreted autonomously so as to allow member states to maintain exclusions which are general and absolute in scope and which apply to all expenditure. The UK has intervened on behalf of France.

18.   C-58/96 : Belgium -v- Commission

Same as Case C-407/95 although in relation to a different reference period.

19.   C-123/96 : Spain -v- Commission

Spain challenges Commission Regulation 92/2, which is based on Article 90(3) and amends Commission Regulation 90/388 with regard to the mobile and personal telecommunications sector. The UK has intervened in support of the Commission in defence of the Regulation.

20.   C-124/96 : Commission -v- Spain

The UK has intervened in support of Spain as we disagree with the Commission's interpretation of Article 13A of the Sixth VAT Directive.

21.   *C-170/96 : Commission -v- Council

These annulment proceedings relate to the Act of the Council of 4 March 1996 on joint action on airport transit arrangements which was adopted using the legal base of Article K3. The Commission contends that the matters governed by the Act fall within the competence of the Community and not within the third pillar.

22.   C-195/96 : Germany -v- Commission

Related to Case C-399/95.

23.   C-199/96 : Spain -v- Commission

Spain challenges Commission Regulation 96/19, which is based on Article 90(3) and concerns the implementation of full competition in the telecommunications sector. The UK has intervened in support of the Commission in defence of the Regulation.

24.   C-217/96 : Belgium -v- Commission

Same as case C-407/95 although in relation to a different reference period.

25.   C-285/96 : Commission -v- Italy

Directive 76/464 on pollution caused by certain dangerous substances discharged into the aquatic environment of the Community. The UK has intervened in support of Italy.

26.   *C-301/96 : Germany -v- Commission
This case and Cases C-302/96, T-132/96 and T-143/96 concern the Commission's refusal to authorise the grant of state aid to Volkswagen plants in Mosel and Chemitz. The UK has applied to intervene in support of the Commission.

27.   *C-302/96 : Commission -v- Germany
See Case C-301/96 above.

(vi) Actions in which the United Kingdom intervened in the Court of First Instance under Article 37 of the Protocol on the Statute of the Court of Justice

1.   T-260/94 : Air-Inter -v- Commission
Regulation 2408/92: application to annul Commission Decision 94/290/EEC that the French policy on the distribution of traffic between airports results in discrimination based on the nationality of air carriers. Judgment 19 June. See Part 2 of this Appendix.

2.   T-371/94 : B A -v- Commission
State Aids : Air France.

3.   T-374/95 : European Night Services Ltd -v- Commission
Articles 85 & 86 of the EC Treaty - Joint Venture by railway companies in respect of rail services via the Channel Tunnel - Commission granted limited exemption under Article 85 - challenge to conditions imposed.

4.   T-375/95 : European Passenger Services Ltd -v- Commission
See T-374/95

5.   T-384/94 : UIC & NS -v- Commission
See T-374/95.

6.   T-388/94 : SNCF -v- Commission
See T-374/95.

7.   T-394/94 : British Midlands Air Ways Ltd -V- Commission
State Aids : Air France.

8.   T-11/95 : BP -v- Commission
Article 93 of the EC Treaty - State aid to Italian chemicals industry - injection of capital - market investor principle.

9.   T-105/95 : WWF UK -v- Commission
An application to annul a Commission decision rejecting access to certain documents. Judgment 5 March.

10.   T-110/95 : IECC -v- Commission
Articles 85 and 86 - Commission investigation of a complaint regarding arrangements between Post Offices in the member states concerning remail services.

11.   T-133/95 : IECC -v- Commission
See T-110/95.

12.   T-174/95 : Swedish Journalists -v- Council
Disclosure of documents.

13.   T-204/95 : IECC -v- Commission
See T-10/95 and T-133/95.

14.   T-234/95 : Hamburger Stahlwerke -v- Commission
An application to annul a Commission Decision on state aid granted to the German Steel industry.

15.   T-2/96 : Neue Maxhütte Stahlwerke -v- Commission
Linked to case T-234/95.

16.   T-42/96 : Primex -v- Commission
The applicant importer challenges a Commission decision not to grant remission of Customs duties on the importation of certain consignments of Hilton beef into Germany when the Certificate of Authority as to the origin and quality of the goods was proved to be forged through no fault of the importer. The UK has intervened in support of the importer.

17.   T-50/96 : Eyckler -v- Commission
See T-42/96.

18.   T-96/96 : Telecom Italia -v- Commission
Telecom Italia challenges Commission Regulation 96/19 which is based on Article 90(3) and concerns the implementation of full competition in the telecommunications sector. The UK has intervened in support of the Commission.

19.   T-97/96 : Neue Maxhutte Stahlwerke GmbH -v- Commission
Related to case T-2/96.

20.   T-102/96 : Gencor -v- Commission
The applicant challenges a Commission decision finding a concentration to be incompatible with the Common Market. The UK has intervened in support of the Commission.

21.   *T-125/96 : Boehringer Ingelheim Vetmedica GmbH and C H Boehringer Sohn Limited Partnership -v- Council
This is an action for damages in respect of loss caused by the adoption of a Council Directive prohibiting the marketing of certain products. The UK has intervened in support of the Applicants in order to take issue with the Council's submission that any such proceedings should be directed at member states whose implementation of the Directive will be the proximate cause of Applicant's loss.

22.   *T-132/96 : Freistaat Sachsen -v- Commission
See Case C-301/96 above.

23.   *T-143/96 : Volkswagen AG & Volkswagen Sachsen -v- Commission
See Case C-301/96 above.

24.   *T-6/97 : Comafrica SpA and Dole Fresh Fruit Europe Ltd & Co. -v- Commission
The UK has intervened in support of the Commission in this challenge to method of calculating the Applicants' entitlement to licences for the import into the Community of third country bananas.

(vii) Cases referred to the European Court under the Judgments convention

1.   C-163/95 : Von Horn -v- Cinnamond
Brussels Convention - proceedings instituted in Portugal before that country became a Contracting State - jurisdiction of the English courts in respect of proceedings brought subsequently in England.

2.   C-295/95 : Farrell -v- Long
Whether Article 5(2) of the Brussels Convention requires as a condition precedent to the Institution of Maintenance proceedings that a maintenance creditor should have already obtained an order for maintenance against the main creditor. Judgment 20 March.

3.   C-391/95 - Van Uden Maritime
Brussels Convention - scope for the Arbitration Exception and whether this extends to proceedings for interim or protective relief.

4.   C-122/96 : Saldhana
Concerns the power of the Austrian courts to make orders for security for costs against a plaintiff who is a national of another EU State (although the action pre-dates Austria's accession to the EU) in circumstances where the plaintiff's assets are held in a third country, and the Austrian Court's judgment will be enforced in that third country. This is a follow-on from Data Delecta.

5.   C-126/96 : Brizard -v- Grant
Whether, under the Brussels Convention, an enforcing court should order a stay or security for costs pending the outcome of an appeal in the originating court's jurisdiction. Withdrawn.

(viii)   Requests for an Opinion of the European Court of Justice under Article 228(1) of the EEC Treaty.

None.

(ix) Actions against United Kingdom under Article 170.

None.

(x) Appeals from the CFI to the ECJ

1.   *C-55/97P : AIUFFASS & AKT -v- Commission
The Appellants in this case ask the Court to overrule the judgment of the CFI dismissing their application for annulment of the Commission Decision which authorised the UK to grant aid to the Hualon Corporation for the establishment of a textiles factory in Northern Ireland.

CFI Case T260/94: Air Inter SA -v- Commission of the European Communities (Judgment 19 June)

1.   This case involved an application to annul Commission Decision 94/291 requiring France to stop refusing Community air carriers traffic rights on the Paris (Orly) to Marseille and Toulouse routes, which was to the advantage of Air Inter alone, in breach of Regulation 2408/92. French authorities had refused TAT European Airlines' applications for access to Orly on the ground that Article 5 of Regulation 2408/92 authorized the continuation of the exclusive concession granted to Air Inter. The UK intervened in support of the Commission.

2.   The CFI held that Air Inter did not hold an exclusive concession on domestic routes between Paris and Marseille or Toulouse. "Routes" means routes between two cities or regions, and Orly and Charles de Gaulle, to which TAT flew, form the "airport system" for Paris. TAT were therefore discriminated against in breach of Regulation 2408/92. Air Inter was not able to benefit from the derogation in Article 90(2) of the EC Treaty, which must be strictly interpreted, because it failed to show that the Decision would obstruct its ability, in law or fact, to cross-subsidize from the profitable Orly routes to unprofitable domestic routes. Finally, the contested Decision was not disproportionate because the Regulation was correctly applied.

ECJ Joined Cases C304/94; C330/94; C342/94 and C224/95 Tombesi and others (known as "Savini") (Judgment 25 June)

1.   These cases were referred by two Italian courts and involved criminal proceedings against a number of individuals accused of various offences relating to the transporting and disposal of waste.

2.   The Court was asked to rule on the interpretation of a number of EC waste directives including Council Directive 75/442/EEC, as amended by Council Directive 91/156/EEC ("the waste framework directive"). In Savini, in which the UK intervened, the national court expressed its doubts about the compatibility with EC waste legislation of provisions of Italian law removing certain substances from the scope of national controls on waste. The Italian court asked the ECJ to rule on whether the EC legislation provided for the exclusion from the definition of waste of substances and objects which were capable of economic reutilisation and on whether the concept of waste in EC legislation includes substances which would be reutilised and which were the subject of a legal transaction or were quoted on private and commercial lists.

3.   The case aroused considerable interest in certain sectors of industry, in particular the scrap metals industry.

4.   Noting that Article 1(a) of the waste framework directive, as amended, laid down a common definition of waste which applied, inter alia, to shipments of waste within member states, the Court referred to earlier case law, in particular Case C359/88 Zanetti and Case C442/92 Commission v Germany in which it had ruled that the concept of waste in the original versions of the waste framework directive and hazardous waste directive did not

exclude substances or objects which were capable of economic reutilisation. National law which provided for such exclusions was not therefore compatible with those directives. That interpretation had not been altered by the subsequent amendments to those directives which had simply reinforced the system of supervision over the handling of waste. It followed that the waste framework directive, as amended, covered all objects and substances discarded by their owners even if they had a commercial value, were collected on a commercial basis for recycling, reclamation or re-use, were the subject of a transaction or were quoted on public or private commercial lists.

5.   It had been hoped by some, particularly in industry, that the Court would take the opportunity in these cases to elaborate to some degree on the principle laid down in Zanetti and other cases so as to clarify the scope of the definition of waste in EC waste legislation. In the end however, the Court has done little more than reaffirm the same broad principle established in Zanetti: that substances or objects are not excluded from the definition of waste (and do not therefore fall outside the special controls on waste) simply because they are capable of being reused on a commercial basis.

ECJ Case C313/94: Ayse Suzen -v- Zehnacker Gebaudereinigung Gmbh Krankenhausservice, Lefarth Gmbh (Judgment 11 March)

1.   The reference asked whether the termination of a cleaning contract and the transfer of that contract to another undertaking constituted a transfer of a business within the meaning of the Directive 77/187/EEC -on the safeguarding of employee's rights in the event of transfers of undertakings, businesses of parts of businesses.

2.   The Court held that a transfer within the meaning of the Directive takes place if the economic entity retains its identity. An "entity" refers to an organised grouping of persons and assets facilitating the exercise of an economic activity which pursues a specific objective.   In order to determine whether the conditions for a "transfer of an entity" are met, the national court should take into account factors such as whether there was a transfer of substantial tangible or intangible assets, and whether the new employer has taken over a major part of the workforce in terms of numbers and skills.

3.   The Court emphasised that the loss of a service to a competitor cannot indicate by itself the existence of a transfer within the meaning of the Directive. In those circumstances the service undertaking previously entrusted with the contract does not, on losing a customer, thereby cease to exist and a business or part of a business belonging to it cannot be considered to have been transferred to the new awardee of the contract.

4.   This case illustrates that the application of the Directive should be considered on a case-by-case basis turning on the overall balance of factors set out above.

ECJ Case C2/95: Sparekassernes Datacenter (SDC) -v- Skatteministereriet (Judgment 5 June)

1.   This was a reference to the ECJ by a Danish court. It concerned the extent of some of the exemptions provided for by Article 13.B(d) of Council Directive 77/388/EEC relating to the common system of value added tax.

2.   The transactions in question are of the type usually performed by financial institutions, for example, transactions concerning current accounts and payments, and transactions in shares. The ECJ decided that the exemptions in question are not limited to certain classes of trader or means of effecting the transaction. For example, a data-handling centre makes an exempt transaction if its operation is distinct in character and specific to, and essential for, a payment.

3.   The case is important in the context of advancing technology and contracting out of functions by traders in the financial sector. There may be a narrow borderline between contributing to an exempt transaction and actually making one.

ECJ Cases C9/95, C23/95 And C156/95: Belgium and Germany -v- Commission (Judgment 4 February)

1.   In September 1994, Tropical Storm Debbie severely damaged banana plantations in the French Overseas Departments of Martinique and Guadeloupe and the Caribbean States of Saint Lucia and Dominica, which enjoy preferential access to the Community for their bananas. In response, the Commission increased the tariff quota for imports of "dollar" bananas (from Central and South America) and allocated the increase to the banana suppliers affected. Germany and Belgium challenged the relevant regulations, claiming that the Commission could not increase the tariff quota unless it distributed the increase among the totality of banana suppliers, according to the general rule on quota increases laid down in the common organisation of the market in bananas.

2.   The ECJ held that the regulations were not covered by the Commission's power to adopt transitional measures; but were validly based on a delegated power to increase the tariff quota in response to "exceptional circumstances affecting production and import conditions". In such circumstances, the Commission could depart from the general rule on quota increases, without exceeding the implementation powers conferred by the Council. Under the Common Agricultural Policy, the Council can confer wide powers on the Commission, which is then authorised to adopt all measures necessary or appropriate for the implementation of the basic legislation.

3.   The Judgment elucidates the scope of the powers which the Council may confer on the Commission under Article 155 of the EC Treaty, particularly in relation to agriculture, and throws light on the concept of transitional measures.

ECJ Case C27/95: Woodspring District Council -v- Bakers of Nailsea Limited (Judgment 15 April)

1.   Council Directive 91/497/EEC, which consolidates Community rules on meat hygiene, requires that inspections at slaughterhouses be carried out by official veterinarians and that animals be inspected ante-mortem. Related Community rules require that inspection costs be paid by the slaughterhouse. In this case, a slaughterhouse argued that these provisions infringed Articles 39 and 40(3) of the EC Treaty and the principles of proportionality and equal treatment.

2.   The ECJ found that the Community rules accorded with the objectives of the Common Agricultural Policy (CAP) and Article 39 and did not discriminate against Bakers contrary to Article 40(3); nor were they disproportionate. Official veterinarians could reasonably be regarded as best qualified to carry out inspections; ante-mortem inspections were needed to diagnose diseases only apparent in live animals; and slaughterhouses could be made financially responsible for inspections, as these guaranteed the hygiene of their products. With all three measures, the Council had correctly exercised the wide discretionary power it enjoyed under the CAP, given that none was manifestly inappropriate.

3.   The Judgment illustrates how the ECJ assesses the validity of Community legislation on the CAP, and establishes that, unlike member states, the Community need not charge the cost of hygiene inspections to the general public.

ECJ Cases C65/95 and C111/95: Shingara and Radiom (Judgment 17 June)

1.   A reference from the High Court to the European Court of Justice under Article 177. The case is concerned with the exclusion from the UK of a French national and the removal of a dual Irish/Iranian national both on the grounds that their presence here was not conducive to the public good.

2.   The applicants sought to rely on Directive 64/221/EEC, which deals with the co-ordination of special measures concerning the movement and residence of foreign nationals, which are justified on grounds of public policy, public security or public health. In particular, they invoked Articles 8 and 9, which deal with rights of appeal against refusals of entry, refusals to issue or renew a residence permit and orders of expulsion.

3.   The Court concluded that Article 8 required nationals of other member states to be granted the same remedies available against acts of the administration generally in that member state. This involved effectively rejecting the Government's contention that judicial review (the only legal remedy available to the applicants) was sufficient in the context of the Directive. Because the decision to exclude the applicants from the UK had been taken on the grounds of national security, they enjoyed no statutory appeal capable of determining the merits of their cases.

4.   In response to the judgments, the Government has introduced the Special Immigration Appeals Commission Bill which will confer a right of appeal on those in the position of the applicants in this case.

ECJ Case C66/95 : R -v- Secretary of State for Social Security Ex Parte Eunice Sutton (Judgment 22 April)

1.   Mrs Sutton was awarded Invalid Care Allowance (ICA) belatedly and arrears paid. The award followed another case where the ECJ had held that UK rules debarring women aged 60 to 64 from ICA, contravened Council Directive 79/7/EEC (equality of treatment between men and women in social security matters). Mrs Sutton then requested payment of interest on the arrears. When the Secretary of State refused to pay interest she sought a judicial review of that decision. The High Court referred the matter to the ECJ for a judgment as to whether an individual should be able to obtain interest on arrears of a social security benefit when the delay in payment is due to discrimination prohibited by Community law.

2.   In answering that question the ECJ drew a clear distinction between entitlement to benefit and the reparation for loss or damage sustained because of discrimination, contrary to Community Law. By way of example, a person experiencing discriminatory dismissal from employment sud entitled to interest on the amount payable as an essential component of compensation for the purpose of restoring real equality of treatment, was in a different position from a person claiming a social security benefit. The ECJ also re-iterated, as a matter of-general principle, that a member state is liable for loss and damage caused to an individual as a result of breaches in Community law. It is, however, for the national court to determine whether and how that obligation should be discharged, so long as the reparation was not less favourable than if made in accordance with domestic provisions.

ECJ Case C124/95: R -v- HM Treasury and the Bank of England ex parte Centro-Com SRl (Judgment 14 January)

1.   This was a reference to the ECJ by the Civil Division of the Court of Appeal. It concerned two questions on the interpretation of Articles 113 and 234 of the Treaty and

Council Regulation (EEC)1432/92 prohibiting trade between the EC and the Republic of Serbia and Montenegro. The Regulation implemented on behalf of the Community a UN Sanctions Resolution.

2.   The Court held that member states were precluded by the Regulation from adopting measures to allow payment in respect of exports to be made only if the exports had been made from their own territory.

3.   The Court further found that national measures contrary to Article 113 could be justified under Article 234 only if necessary to ensure that the member state concerned performed its obligations towards non member states under an agreement concluded prior to entry into force of the Treaty or the accession of the member state concerned.

4.   The case is important in that it clarifies the relationship between member states and the Community in implementing UN Security Council Resolutions.

ECJ Case C177/95: Ebony Maritime (Judgment 27 February)

1.   This case involved the interpretation of certain provisions of Council Regulation No.990/93 and Decision 93/235/ECSC, both dated 26 April 1993, concerning trade with the Former Republic of Yugoslavia (FRY). These implemented elements of UN Security Council sanctions resolutions against the FRY.

2.   A Maltese registered tanker bound for Croatia carrying petroleum products belonging to Ebony Maritime, a Liberian company, was boarded by NATO/WEU forces in a sanctions enforcement operation. As the vessel was shipping water, it headed for Montenegro. It was boarded before it entered Yugoslav territorial waters and was towed to Brindisi where it was impounded and the cargo was confiscated, following a decision of the Prefect of Brindisi under Italian law. Ebony Maritime and the tanker's owners, Loten Navigation, sought to annul his decision.

3.   The Italian Court asked the ECJ whether the prohibition on maritime commercial traffic from entering the FRY's territorial waters set out in the Regulation and the Decision only operated when a vessel entered those waters, or whether it also operated when the vessel was in international waters but there were good grounds for believing that it would be entering territorial waters. The ECJ decided that the prohibition would bite if the vessel concerned was in international waters but appeared to be on course for territorial waters for commercial purposes even if it were flying the flag of a non-member state and belonged, together with its cargo, to non-Community companies. The Decision was inapplicable because trade in petroleum products falls outside the ECSC Treaty.

4.   The Court also asked whether domestic legislation prescribing confiscation of the cargo in the event of a breach of a prohibition in Article 1 was compatible with the Regulation. The ECJ upheld member state competence to determine the penalties to be imposed under domestic law for such breach. It was not contrary to proportionality for the cargo's owner to be penalised in the same way as the vessel's owner, regardless of their respective degrees of involvement in the breach. It was for the national court to decide whether a penalty complied with EC law and, in particular, was dissuasive, effective and proportionate, taking into account that the Regulation's objective was of fundamental interest to the international community.

Case C300/95: Commission -v- United Kingdom (Judgment 29 May)

1.   The Commission claimed that the UK had failed properly to implement Council Directive 85/374/EEC (the product liability directive). The Product Liability Directive requires

member states to provide that producers shall be strictly liable for damage caused by defects in their products. The Directive sets out a number of defences, one of which provides that the producer will not be liable if he proves that "the state of scientific and technical knowledge at the time when he put the product into circulation was not such as to enable the existence of the defect to be discovered". This is known as the "development risks defence".

2.   The Directive is implemented in the UK by Part I of the Consumer Protection Act 1987. The wording of the development risks defence in section 4(1)(e) of that Act differs from that in the Directive. The Commission claimed that the scope of the defence was broader than the Directive allowed and that the UK had effectively converted the strict liability regime of the Directive into mere liability for negligence.

3.   The Court dismissed the Commission's application. It held that the Commission had failed to support its application by reference to any decision of the UK courts which interpreted the Act inconsistently with the Directive.

4.   The case emphasises that the scope of national laws must be assessed in the light of the interpretation given to them by national courts.

ECJ Case C343/95: Diego Calì & Figli Srl -v- Servizi Ecologici Porto di Genova SpA (Judgment 18 March)

1.   This case involved an Article 177 reference from the Tribunale di Genova regarding the interpretation of Article 86 of the EC Treaty. It arose from a dispute between the parties about the charges levied by SEPG for compulsory preventive anti-pollution services which it performed in the port of Genoa-Multedo.

2.   The ECJ distinguished between situations where the State exercised official authority and where it carried on economic activities of an industrial or commercial nature by offering goods or services on the market. In drawing the distinction, the ECJ considered the nature of the activities carried out by SEPG (on whom the State had conferred an exclusive right). The ECJ concluded that its pollution prevention activities, as opposed to it activities in cleaning up pollution, were carried out in the public interest and formed part of the essential functions of the State as regards protection of the environment. They were not of an economic nature. Furthermore, the ECJ held that the levying of a charge for its pollution prevention measures was an integral part of SEPG's surveillance activity and cannot affect the legal status of that activity. Therefore, the ECJ held, these activities did not come within the scope of Article 86.

ECJ Case C400/95: Handels-og Kontorfunktion(rernes Forbund I Danmark, Acting on behalf of Helle Elisabeth Larsson -v- Dansk Handel and Service, Acting on behalf of Fotex Supermarked A/S (Judgment 29 May)

1.   Ms Larsson became pregnant and subsequently developed a pregnancy-related illness. She was on continuous sick leave for 19 weeks until her maternity leave began in March 1992. When her leave ended on 16 October 1992 she was still unfit for work. Her employment was terminated for sickness absence at the end of December. She complained that she had been dismissed because of her pregnancy, contrary to the Equal Treatment Directive (76/207/EEC) which prohibits sex discrimination.

2.   The Court ruled that the Directive did not require illnesses arising out of pregnancy or confinement to be treated differently from other kinds of illness. Absence from work for maternity reasons was protected by the specific rules on maternity leave adopted by member states. Accordingly, an employer could not take account of any illness during the period of

maternity leave. Apart from that, the Directive did not prevent an employer, when applying its normal, non-discriminatory rules on dismissal for sickness absence, from taking into account periods of pregnancy-related illness that occurred between the onset of pregnancy and the beginning of maternity leave.

3.   The decision resolved an important issue: previous decisions by the Court had been seen by many commentators as meaning that it was unlawful sex discrimination to dismiss for maternity-related illness, except in the case where the illness continued after the end of maternity leave. Directive 92/85/EEC on the protection of pregnant workers now sets minimum standards for maternity protection, including a general prohibition on dismissal for reasons connected with pregnancy (implemented in Part X of the Employment Rights Act 1996).

ECJ Case C14/96: Paul Denuit (Judgment 29 May)

1.   In this case the ECJ was asked by the Belgian Court of First Instance for a preliminary ruling on three questions on the interpretation of the EC Broadcasting Directive (89/552/EEC). The Directive is a single market instrument intended to allow the free movement of television broadcasting throughout the Community, subject to certain minimum standards which are the responsibility of the member state having jurisdiction over a broadcaster.

2.   Mr Paul Denuit, the managing director of a Belgian cable broadcasting distributor, had been the subject of criminal proceedings under domestic Belgian broadcasting law for allowing the retransmission by cable of the television channels TNT and Cartoon Network. These channels were originally broadcast by Turner Broadcasting under a licence granted by the UK broadcasting regulator, the Independent Television Commission. Turner Broadcasting is established in the UK.

3.   The Belgian court considered that there was a lack of clarity over which country had jurisdiction over these services, and that as they did not meet the Directive's requirement that a majority of their programming should be of European origin, the Belgian authorities were entitled to take measures to restrict retransmission of the services on the Belgian cable network. The ECJ was asked:

- what criteria should be applied in determining the country of jurisdiction, and whether the proportion of European works broadcast had a bearing on the question of jurisdiction;

- under what conditions a member state could take measures to restrict or prohibit retransmission of a broadcaster authorised to broadcast by another member state, where that broadcaster did not come under the jurisdiction of the second member state;

- whether a member state could take measures to oppose retransmission on its territory of a service which was not effectively required by the member state with jurisdiction over the broadcaster to comply with the quota provisions of the Directive.

4.   The Court ruled that the place of establishment of the broadcaster was the determinant of the member state having jurisdiction over that broadcaster, and that the extent to which particular broadcasters complied with the quota provisions of the Directive was irrelevant in determining jurisdiction. It also ruled that the fact that a broadcaster had not complied with the quota provisions of the Directive did not entitle the receiving member state to take measures to restrict retransmission on its territory.

5.   The immediate effect of the judgment is that TNT and Cartoon Network should be allowed unrestricted retransmission in Belgium. The broader impact is that all broadcasters properly licensed in the UK will have unfettered access to the broadcasting market throughout

the Community, as no member state should restrict retransmission of such services on their domestic cable networks.

ECJ Case C114/96: Kieffer and Thill

1.   This was a reference to the Court under Article 177 of the EC Treaty by the Tribunal de Police, Luxembourg for a preliminary ruling in the criminal proceedings before the court against Rene Kieffer and Romain Thill. The Tribunal de Police asked whether, in requiring member states to collect a detailed declaration of all intra Community imports and exports from traders exceeding stipulated thresholds (the Intrastat system), Council Regulation 3330/91 introduced a measure having an equivalent effect to a quantitative restriction on trade in goods between member states prohibited by Articles 30 and 34 of the EEC Treaty and whether the obligation contained in the regulation constitutes an unjustified and disproportionate constraint on traders contrary to Article 3b.

2.   The ECJ ruled that examination of Council Regulation (EEC) 3330/91 on the statistics relating to the trading of goods between member states did not disclose any factors which cast doubt on its validity - an important decision as regards the integrity of the Intrastat system.

Appendix E: House of Commons Debates on European Community Documents

Date   Subject and Document References

a. European Standing Committee A

1.   12 February   Commission Report on Raw Tobacco (5217/97)

2.   19 February   Future Noise Policy (11419/96)

b. European Standing Committee B

1.   15 January   European Community Budget (9372/96, SEC(96)
                          1677, P, E, 252, 724, Unnumbered EMs submitted by
                          Treasury on 15 and 29 November 1996)

2.   29 January   Resale right for the benefit of the author of an
                          original work of art (7050/96)

3.   12 February   Company Law: Takeover Bids (5147/96)

4.   5 March   Court of Auditors Report 1995/96 Statement of
                          Assurance for 1995 (OJ C340, OJ C395)

5.   19 March   Structural Funds/Cohesion Policy (11382/96,
                          12614/96)

Appendix F: Reports from the House of Lords Select Committee on the European Communities

a. Reports Presented for Debate

1. Community Railway Strategy - 9654/96 (COM(96)421) — 7th Report (1996-97) 18 February

2. Consumer Guarantees - 9643/96 (COM(96)520) — 10th Report (1996-97) 4 March

3. Reducing disparities within the European Union: the effectiveness of the Structural and Cohesion Funds - 5494/96 (COM(96)109) — 11th Report (1996-97) 18 March

4. EC Tobacco Regime - 5217/97 (COM(96) 554) — 13th Report (1996-97) 19 March

b. Report Presented for Information

1. Evidence by the Minister of State, FCO, on the Dublin European Council and related matters — 6th Report (1996-97) 4 February

2. Production and Marketing of Honey - 12197/96 and Supplementary Memo (COM(96)596) — 8th Report (1996-97) 4 March

3. Revisions to the EC Broadcasting Directive - 12609/96 (COM(96)626) — 9th Report (1996-97) 4 March

4. Correspondence with Ministers — 12th Report (1996-97) 18 March

5. Europol: Confidentiality Regulations - (P) 11143/96, (P) 5858/97 — 1st Report (1997-98) 17 June

c. Debates Held

1. Takeover Bids - 5147/96 (COM(95)655) — 13th Report (1996-97) 14 January

2. EC Tobacco Regime - 5217/97 (COM(96)554) — 13th Report (1996-97) 9 June

3. Consumer Guarantees - 9643/96 (COM(96)520) 10 June — 10th Report (1996-97)

4. Community Railway Strategy - 9654/96 (COM(96)421) — 7th Report (1996-97) 12 June

Appendix G: United Kingdom Trade with other Member States of the European Union

All figures are on a balance of payments basis.

Importance of Trade within the EU

Around 55 per cent of the United Kingdom's trade (exports plus imports) is now with other member states, compared with about 40 per cent prior to United Kingdom membership. In recent years Germany has become our most important trading partner and eight of our top ten markets are members of the Community.

Trade Performance in the EU

In the first half of 1997 United Kingdom trade with other member states amounted to £95.7 billion compared with £96.8 billion in the first half of 1996. Exports and imports each fell by (per cent.

By Commodity

In January to June 1997 exports of fuels (mainly oil) accounted for 8 per cent of our total exports to other member states, up from 7 per cent in the same period a year earlier but well below the figure of nearly 30 per cent in the mid-1980s. This declining share can to some extent be explained by weaker oil prices in subsequent years. The surplus on fuels rose by £0.8 billion to £3.2 billion.

The deficit on manufactured goods rose by £0.3 billion to £2.1 billion.

UNITED KINGDOM TRADE WITH THE EUROPEAN COMMUNITY £ billion, Balance of Payments Basis

	Total Trade				Food, Beverages and Tobacco				Basic Materials			
	Exports	Imports	Balance	Export/ Import Ratio %	Exports	Imports	Balance	Export/ Import Ratio %	Exports	Imports	Balance	Export/ Import Ratio%
1970	3.2	3.1	+0.1	104	0.1	0.8	-0.6	19	0.2	0.3	-0.1	63
1971	3.4	3.7	-0.2	94	0.2	0.9	-0.7	18	0.2	0.3	-0.1	65
1972	3.8	4.6	-0.8	83	0.2	1.0	-0.8	21	0.2	0.3	-0.1	69
1973	5.0	6.8	-1.7	75	0.3	1.4	-1.1	22	0.3	0.5	-0.2	60
1974	7.1	9.7	-2.6	73	0.3	2.0	-1.7	14	0.4	0.6	-0.2	61
1975	7.9	10.6	-2.7	75	0.5	2.4	-1.9	21	0.4	0.6	-0.2	67
1976	11.1	13.7	-2.6	81	0.6	2.5	-1.9	25	0.6	0.9	-0.3	68
1977	14.2	16.4	-2.2	87	0.9	2.9	-2.0	31	0.7	1.0	-0.3	69
1978	15.9	18.7	-2.8	85	1.3	3.1	-1.8	41	0.7	0.9	-0.2	76
1979	20.5	23.6	-3.1	87	1.4	3.4	-2.1	40	0.9	1.1	-0.2	82
1980	24.2	23.3	+0.9	104	1.5	3.3	-1.8	45	1.1	1.0	+0.1	106
1981	24.5	24.7	-0.2	99	1.6	3.6	-2.0	44	0.9	1.1	-0.3	78
1982	27.2	28.6	-1.5	95	1.7	4.0	-2.3	43	1.0	1.3	-0.3	76
1983	31.4	34.3	-3.0	91	1.8	4.6	-2.7	40	1.1	1.5	-0.4	76
1984	37.0	40.7	-3.7	91	1.9	5.1	-3.1	38	1.5	1.9	-0.4	77
1985	42.2	45.0	-2.8	94	2.1	5.5	-3.4	38	1.6	1.9	-0.3	83
1986	38.4	48.5	-10.1	79	2.7	6.3	-3.6	43	1.5	1.9	-0.4	79
1987	42.7	53.9	-11.2	79	2.7	6.6	-3.8	42	1.6	2.2	-0.7	71
1988	44.5	60.2	-15.7	74	3.3	6.6	-3.3	50	1.4	2.3	-0.9	60
1989	51.2	68.7	-17.5	75	3.8	7.3	-3.5	52	1.6	2.6	-1.0	61
1990	58.7	70.4	-11.7	83	4.1	7.9	-3.8	51	1.6	2.5	-0.9	65
1991	63.0	65.3	-2.4	96	4.8	7.8	-3.0	62	1.4	2.2	-0.8	62
1992	64.8	69.8	-4.9	93	5.5	8.6	-3.1	64	1.2	2.3	-1.0	55
1993	69.0	74.4	-5.3	93	5.6	8.8	-3.2	63	1.4	2.4	-1.0	58
1994	76.9	82.4	-5.6	93	6.3	9.2	-2.9	68	1.7	2.8	-1.1	60
1995	89.5	93.6	-4.1	96	7.1	10.1	-3.0	70	1.9	3.0	-1.1	64
1996	95.0	99.2	-4.0	96	6.9	10.8	-3.9	64	1.7	3.0	-1.2	59
Jan–Jun 96	47.4	49.4	-1.9	96	3.5	5.4	-1.9	65	0.9	1.5	-0.6	61
Jan–Jun 97	47.1	48.6	-1.5	97	3.3	5.3	-2.0	62	0.8	1.4	-0.6	59

	Fuels				Manufactures			
	Exports	Imports	Balance	Export/ Import Ratio %	Exports	Imports	Balance	Export/ Import Ratio %
1970	0.1	0.2	-0.1	53	2.7	1.8	+0.9	149
1971	0.1	0.3	-0.1	49	2.9	2.2	+0.7	131
1972	0.1	0.3	-0.2	45	3.2	2.9	+0.2	108
1973	0.2	0.4	-0.2	50	4.1	4.3	-0.2	95
1974	0.5	1.1	-0.6	45	5.8	6.0	-0.2	97
1975	0.5	1.1	-0.6	48	6.3	6.4	-0.1	98
1976	0.8	1.4	-0.6	60	8.8	8.7	+0.1	102
1977	1.3	1.4	-0.1	94	11.0	10.9	+0.1	101
1978	1.5	1.3	+0.2	115	12.0	13.2	-1.1	91
1979	3.0	2.0	+1.0	149	14.9	16.8	-1.9	89
1980	4.6	2.0	+2.7	234	16.6	16.7	-0.1	99
1981	6.1	2.1	+4.0	285	15.5	17.5	-2.0	88
1982	7.0	2.2	+4.8	323	17.0	20.8	-3.8	82
1983	9.0	2.2	+6.8	409	18.8	25.6	-6.8	73
1984	10.7	3.4	+7.3	317	22.3	29.9	-7.6	75
1985	12.3	3.3	+9.0	371	25.6	33.7	-8.1	76
1986	6.0	1.9	+4.1	315	27.4	37.7	-10.4	73
1987	6.0	1.9	+4.1	317	31.6	42.6	-11.0	74
1988	4.2	1.4	+2.8	304	34.9	49.0	-14.1	71
1989	4.2	1.6	+2.6	259	40.9	56.4	-15.5	72
1990	5.3	1.9	+3.4	277	46.9	57.4	-10.5	82
1991	5.3	1.9	+3.4	281	50.7	52.7	-2.0	96
1992	4.9	1.7	+3.2	294	52.4	56.5	-4.1	93
1993	5.6	1.6	+4.0	359	56.4	61.4	-5.0	92
1994	5.5	1.3	+4.2	414	63.3	68.9	-5.6	92
1995	6.1	1.3	+4.8	475	74.4	79.0	-4.6	94
1996	7.5	1.5	6.0	502	78.6	83.6	-4.7	95
Jan-Jun 96	3.3	0.8	2.4	398	39.7	41.5	-1.8	96
Jan-Jun 97	3.9	0.7	3.2	580	39.0	41.1	-2.1	95

Source: Office for National Statistics

Printed in the UK for The Stationery Office Limited on behalf of the Controller of Her Majesty's Stationery Office
Dd 5067777   11/97   3401/1/76368   Job No. J0031607   46/40464